ANNOUNCING THE H
NOW IN PREPARATION

The edition of *The Complete Works of Frances Ridley Havergal* has five parts:

Volume I *Behold Your King:*
The Complete Poetical Works of Frances Ridley Havergal

Volume II *Whose I Am and Whom I Serve:*
Prose Works of Frances Ridley Havergal

Volume III *Loving Messages for the Little Ones:*
Works for Children by Frances Ridley Havergal

Volume IV *Love for Love: Frances Ridley Havergal:*
Memorials, Letters and Biographical Works

Volume V *Songs of Truth and Love:*
Music by Frances Ridley Havergal and William Henry Havergal

David L. Chalkley, Editor   Dr. Glen T. Wegge, Music Editor

The Music of Frances Ridley Havergal by Glen T. Wegge, Ph.D.

This Companion Volume to the Havergal edition is a valuable presentation of F.R.H.'s extant scores. Except for a very few of her hymn scores published in hymnbooks, most or nearly all of F.R.H.'s scores have been very little—if any at all—seen, or even known of, for nearly a century. What a valuable body of music has been unknown for so long and is now made available to many. Dr. Wegge completed his Ph.D. in Music Theory at Indiana University at Bloomington, and his diligence and thoroughness in this volume are obvious. First an analysis of F.R.H.'s compositions is given, an essay that both addresses the most advanced musicians and also reaches those who are untrained in music; then all the extant scores that have been found are newly typeset, with complete texts for each score and extensive indices at the end of the book. This volume presents F.R.H.'s music in newly typeset scores diligently prepared by Dr. Wegge, and Volume V of the Havergal edition presents the scores in facsimile, the original 19th century scores. (The essay—a dissertation—analysing her scores is given the same both in this Companion Volume and in Volume V of the Havergal edition.)

Dr. Wegge is also preparing all of these scores for publication in performance folio editions.

Frances Ridley Havergal (1836–1879). Solomon Cole painted this portrait in 1845, when she was eight years old.

LITTLE PILLOWS;

OR,

GOOD-NIGHT THOUGHTS FOR THE LITTLE ONES.

MORNING BELLS;

OR,

WAKING THOUGHTS FOR THE LITTLE ONES.

AND

MORNING STARS;

OR,

NAMES OF CHRIST FOR HIS LITTLE ONES.

BY

FRANCES RIDLEY HAVERGAL.

"Knowing her intense desire that Christ should be magnified, whether
by her life or in her death, may it be to His glory
that in these pages she, being dead,
'Yet speaketh ! ' "

Taken from the Edition of *The Complete Works of Frances Ridley Havergal*

David L. Chalkley, Editor   Dr. Glen T. Wegge, Associate Editor

ISBN 978-1-937236-11-3   Library of Congress: 2011940451

Book cover by Sherry Goodwin and David Carter.

Frances Ridley Havergal (1836–1879). Her forty-second birthday was December 14, 1878, and this photograph was taken seven weeks later, on February 1, only four months before her unexpected early death on June 3, 1879.

CONTENTS.

LIST OF ILLUSTRATIONS.

Love for Love.

1 John 4:16.

Knowing that the God on high,
  With a tender Father's grace,
Waits to hear your faintest cry,
  Waits to show a Father's face,—
Stay and think!—oh, should not you
Love this gracious Father too?

Knowing Christ was crucified,
  Knowing that He loves you now
Just as much as when He died
  With the thorns upon His brow,—
Stay and think!—oh, should not you
Love this blessèd Saviour too?

Knowing that a Spirit strives
  With your weary, wandering heart,
Who can change the restless lives,
  Pure and perfect peace impart,—
Stay and think!—oh, should not you
Love this loving Spirit too?

Frances Ridley Havergal

This next hymn was found in *God Is Love; or, Memorials of Little Nony*, a small book published in Volume IV of this Havergal edition. The author of this hymn is not known, likely not F. R. H.

I.

Lord, look upon a little child,
By nature sinful, rude, and wild;
Oh! put Thy gracious hands on me,
And make me all I ought to be.

II.

Make me Thy child, a child of God,
Washed in my Saviour's precious blood;
And my whole heart from sin set free,
A little vessel full of Thee.

III.

A star of early dawn, and bright,
Shining within Thy sacred light;
A beam of light to all around,
A little spot of hallowed ground.

IV.

Dear Jesus, take me to Thy breast,
And bless me that I may be blest;
Both when I wake and when I sleep,
Thy little lamb in safety keep.

LITTLE PILLOWS;

OR,

GOOD-NIGHT THOUGHTS FOR THE LITTLE ONES.

BY

FRANCES RIDLEY HAVERGAL.

TO

SYBIL AND HELENA,

WITH

AUNT FANNY'S LOVE.

CONTENTS.

HOW "LITTLE PILLOWS" CAME TO BE WRITTEN.

A LITTLE GIRL was away from home on a week's visit. We will suppose her name was Ethel. The first night, when she was tucked up in bed, and just ready for a good-night kiss, I said, "Now, shall I give you a little pillow?"

Ethel lifted her head to see what was under it, and said, "I have got one, Auntie!"

"It was another sort of pillow that I meant to give you; I wonder if you will like it?"

So then Ethel saw it was not a question of feathers and pillow-case; still she did not understand, and so she laughed and said, "Do tell me at once, Auntie, what you mean; don't keep me waiting to guess!"

Then I told her that, just as we wanted a nice soft pillow to lay our heads down upon at night, our hearts wanted a pillow too, something to rest upon, some true, sweet word that we might go to sleep upon happily and peacefully. And that it was a good plan always to take a little text for our pillow every night. So she had one that night, and the next night.

The third night I was prevented from coming up till long after Ethel ought to have been asleep. But there were the bright eyes peeping out robin-red-breast fashion, and a reproachful little voice said, "Auntie, you have not given me any little pillow to-night!"

"Then, do you really care about having the little pillows given you, Ethel?"

"Oh, *of course* I do!" was the answer. She did not seem to think there could possibly be any doubt about it. Certainly the way in which she said that "*of course!*" showed that *she* had no doubt about it!

So it seemed that perhaps other little ones would like to have "little pillows" put ready for every night. For even little hearts are sometimes very weary, and want something to rest upon; and a happy little heart, happy in the love of Jesus, will always be glad to have one of His own sweet words to go to sleep upon.

So here are thirty-one "little pillows," not to be used all at once, nor even two at a time, but one for every night in the month. The little texts are so short, that they will need no learning; but when you have read the explanation, you will be able to keep the text quite safely and quite easily in your mind.

Read the little book before you kneel down to say your evening prayers, because I hope what you read will always remind you of something to pray about. And then, when you lie down and shut your eyes, let your heart rest on the "little pillow" till "He giveth His beloved sleep."

When you have read this little book, another will be ready for you, *Morning Bells,*—little chimes of Bible music to wake you up! Some of them will, I hope, ring in your ears all the day, and help you to go happily and brightly through it, following Jesus at every step.

1.

THE INVITATION.

"Come unto Me."—Matthew 11:28.

WHAT kind, sweet words for your pillow to-night! Jesus says them to
you.

"How am I to know?" Well, they are for every one that is weary and heavy
laden. Do not you know what it is to be weary and tired sometimes? Perhaps
you know what it is to feel almost tired of trying to be good—weary with wishing you could be better. So, you see, it is to *you* that He says "Come!"

And if you have not yet come, you are heavy laden too, even if you do not
feel it; because the burden of sin is heavy enough to sink you down into hell,
unless Jesus takes it from you. So it is to you that He says "Come!"

And lest you should think He says it to grown-up people only, He said,
"Suffer the little children to come unto me." Are you a little child? Then it is
to you that He says "Come!"

"If He were here, and if I could see Him, I should like to come." He *is*
here, as really and truly as you are. Suppose your mother and you were in a
dark room together, and she said, "Come to me!" you would not stop to say, "I
would come if I could see you." You would say, "I am coming, mother!" and
you would soon feel your way across the room, and be safe by her side. Not seeing her would not make any difference.

Jesus calls you now, this very night. He is here, in this very room. Now, will
you not say, "I am coming, Lord Jesus!" and ask Him to stretch out His hand
and help you to come, and draw you quite close to Himself?

Yes, to *Himself,* the blessed, beloved Lord Jesus, who loved you and gave
Himself for you, who has waited so patiently for you, who calls you because He
wants you to come and be His own little lamb, and be taken up in His arms and
blessed. Will you keep Him waiting any longer? Will you not "Come"?

> "Will you not come to Him for life?
>   Why will ye die, oh why?
> He gave His life for you, for you!
> The gift is free, the word is true!
>   Will ye not come? Oh why will ye die?"

2.

ACCEPTED.

"Accepted in the Beloved."—Ephesians 1:6.

WHO is "accepted in the Beloved"? *You*, if you have come to your heavenly Father, asking Him to receive you for Jesus Christ's sake. Dear little one, wanting to know that you are saved and forgiven, take all the beautiful comfort and joy of these words! They are for you just as much as for any grown-up person.

Ask Him *now* to give you faith to believe them for yourself, while you try to understand what they really mean for you.

Suppose a king came and proclaimed among a number of poor children that he would take *any* one to stay with him in his beautiful palace, who really wished to go and asked him to take them. Suppose you heard this, and wished the king would take you. Then the king beckons you, and you venture near; and then the prince royal himself comes and leads you up to his father, and tells you to say what you want, and you say, "I do want to go, please take me!" Will the king break his word and *not* take you? Why, in the first place, he *never* breaks his promise. And then he beckoned you himself, and that was what made you go. And then the prince, who is his beloved son, took your hand and brought you; and would the king send the little one away whom he brought? There can be no mistake about it; he cannot have rejected you, and said he will *not* have you, so you *must* be "accepted."

So every one who has come to Jesus even if only a little girl or boy, is "accepted in the Beloved." Accepted, because God has said, "I will receive you." Accepted, because He Himself has called and drawn you, or you never would have wanted to come. Accepted, because the Beloved One has made the way open for you to come by His own blood, and saves *all* that come unto God by Him. Accepted, not because you were worth God's accepting, but "accepted in the Beloved."

> "Safe in the arms of Jesus,
>   Safe on His gentle breast,
> There, by His love o'ershadowed,
>   Sweetly my soul shall rest.
> Hark! 'tis the voice of angels,
>   Borne in a song to me,
> Over the fields of glory,
>   Over the jasper sea."

3.

THE RED HAND.

"I, even I, am He that blotteth out thy transgressions."—Isaiah 43:25.

THERE was once a deaf mute, named John. Though he never heard any other voice, he heard the voice of Jesus, knew it, loved it, and followed it.

One day he told the lady who had taught him, partly on his fingers and partly by signs, that he had had a wonderful dream. God had shown him a great black book; and all John's sins were written in it, so many, so black! And God had shown him hell, all open and fiery, waiting for him, because of all these sins. But Jesus Christ had come and put His *red hand,* red with the blood of His cross, all over the page, and the red hand, the *dear* red hand, had blotted all John's sins out; and when God held up the book to the light, He could not see one left!

Now His sweet word to you to-night is, "I, even I, am He that blotteth out your transgressions." Will you believe it? "Only believe," and "according to your faith it shall be unto you." It is no fancy or mere feeling, but God's truth, that Jesus Christ's blood has been shed,—nothing can alter that; and that His precious blood blotteth out our transgressions; as St. Paul says (Colossians 2:14), "Blotting out the handwriting of ordinances that was against us."

And oh how much there is to blot out!—sins that you have forgotten, and sins that you did not think were sins at all, besides those you know of—to-day, yesterday, all the past days of your little life. And all these written in His book!

Do you want to have them blotted out forever? Do you pray, "Blot out mine iniquities?" do you want to know that they are blotted out? Then take His word about it, and just believe that it is true, and true for you—"I *have* blotted out as a thick cloud thy transgressions, and as a cloud thy sins: return unto me, for I have redeemed thee."

"I am trusting Thee, Lord Jesus,
Trusting only Thee;
Trusting Thee for full salvation,
Great and free.

"I am trusting Thee for cleansing
Through the crimson flood;
Trusting Thee to make me holy
By Thy blood."

4.

GOD'S LOVE.

"I have loved you, saith the Lord."—Malachi 1:2.

I S not this a sweet pillow to rest upon to-night? But a pillow is of no use if you
only look at it; that does not rest you. You must lay your head down upon it,
and then you rest. So, do not only think, "Yes, that is a very nice text"; but believe it, and lay your heart down restfully upon it; and say, "Yes, He loves me!"

How different these words are from what we should have expected! We
should have expected God to say, "I will love you, if you will love me." But no!
He says, "I *have* loved you." Yes, He has loved you already, poor little restless
heart, that wants to be loved! He loves you now, and will love you always.

But you say, "I wish I knew whether He loves *me!*" Why, He *tells* you so;
and what could He say more? There it stands—"I have loved you, saith the
Lord." It is TRUE, and you need only believe it, and be glad of it, and tell Him
how glad you are that He loves you.

But you say, "Yes, I know He loves good people; but I am so naughty!"
Then He has a special word for you: "God commendeth His love toward us,
in that, while we were yet sinners, Christ died for us." He says nothing about
"good people," but tells you that He loved you so much, while you were naughty, that He has sent the Lord Jesus, His own dear, dear Son, to die for you.
Could He do more than that?

He says in the same verse (Malachi 1:2), "*Yet* ye say, Wherein hast thou
loved us?" *Wherein? O herein!* not that you loved God, but that He loved you,
and sent His Son to suffer instead of you.

When you lie down, think how many answers you can find to that question, "Wherein hast Thou loved us?" See how many proofs of His love you
can count up; and then go to sleep on this soft, safe pillow, "I have loved you,
saith the Lord!"

> "I am so glad that our Father in heaven
> Tells of His love in the book He has given,
> Wonderful things in the Bible I see:
> This is the dearest, that Jesus loves me.

> "Oh, if there's only one song I can sing
> When in His beauty I see the great King;
> This shall my song in eternity be,
> 'Oh, what a wonder, that Jesus loves me!'"

5.

GOD'S CARE.

"He that keepeth thee will not slumber."—Psalm 121:3.

SOMETIMES little children wake in the night, and feel lonely, and a little bit afraid. This is not because of the darkness; for if others are with them, talking and moving about, they do not mind it at all. But it is the stillness, the strange silence when everybody is fast asleep.

Everybody? No! The One who loves you best of all is watching you all the time; the One who careth for you never sleeps—"He that keepeth thee will not slumber." He is there all the time, never leaving you one moment alone, never going away at all. It makes no difference to Him that it is very dark, for "the darkness and the light are both alike to Thee." And all through the dark hours He "keepeth thee"; keeps you from everything that could hurt or even frighten you, so that you may safely and quietly take the sweet sleep He gives you.

He "keepeth thee"; only think who is your Keeper! the mighty God, who can do everything, and can see everything. Why need you ever fear with such a Keeper? It is very nice to know that "He shall give His angels charge over thee to keep thee"; but it is sweeter and grander still to think that God Himself keeps us. As if He wanted us to be very sure of it, and to leave us no excuse for ever being afraid any more, He even says it three times over, "He that keepeth thee will not slumber." "Behold, He that keepeth Israel shall neither slumber nor sleep." "The Lord is thy Keeper." What could He say more?

Now what will you say to Him if you wake in the night and feel lonely in the stillness? Will you not recollect what a pillow He has given you to-night to rest upon, and say to Him, "I will trust, and not be afraid"?

> "He will take care of you! All through the night
> Jesus, the Shepherd, His little one keeps:
> Darkness to Him is the same as the light;
> He never slumbers and He never sleeps."

6.

WHAT CHRIST BORE FOR US.

"The Lord hath laid on Him the iniquity of us all."—Isaiah 53:6.

WHERE are your sins? Wherever they are, God's terrible punishment must fall. Even if there were only one sin, and that one hidden away down in your heart, God's wrath must find it out, and punish it. It could not escape.

But you know of many more than one; and God knows of more still. And so the great question for you is, Where are they? If He finds them on you, His wrath must fall on you. But if they are put *somewhere else,* you are safe, for He loves you, and only hates your sins. Where can that wonderful "somewhere else" be? To-night's text tells you that God laid them on Jesus. Why did His terrible wrath fall on His beloved, holy Son? Because He had laid our sins on Jesus, and Jesus took them, and was willing to bear them, so that all the dreadful punishment might fall on Him instead of us. Instead of *you,* dear little one!

When the great drops of blood fell down to the ground from His beloved head in Gethsemane, it was because the Lord had laid on Him *your* iniquity. When He hung by His pierced hands and feet upon the cross, alone in the great darkness of God's wrath, it was because He was bearing *your* punishment, because *your* sins were laid upon Him, so that they might not be found upon you, and punished upon you.

Satan will try to persuade you not to believe that *your* sins were laid upon Him, and will try to keep you always doubting it; but God says they were! Which will you believe?

Again look at the solemn question; "Where are your sins?" and then look at Jesus, suffering and dying for you, and answer boldly, "On Jesus! for 'the Lord hath laid on Him the iniquity of us all.'"

> "And so He died! And this is why
> He came to be a man and die:
> The Bible says He came from heaven,
> That we might have our sins forgiven.
>
> "He knew how wicked men had been,
> He knew that God must punish sin;
> So, out of pity, Jesus said,
> He'd bear the punishment instead."

7.

PEACE THROUGH BLOOD.

"Peace through the blood of His cross."—Colossians 1:20.

IF you had been disobedient and naughty to your dear mother, you would feel that there was something between you and her, like a little wall built up between you. Even though you knew she loved you and went on doing kind things for you as usual, you would not be happy with her; you would keep away from her, and it would be a sorrowful day both for her and for you. For there would be no sweet, bright peace between her and you, and no pleasant and untroubled peace in your own heart.

The Lord Jesus knew that it was just like this with us, that there was something between us and God instead of peace, and this something was sin. And there never could be or can be any peace with God while there is sin, so of course there never could be any real peace in our hearts. We could never take away this wall of sin; on the contrary, left to ourselves, we only keep building it higher and higher by fresh sins every day. And God has said, that "without shedding of blood there is no remission," that is, no forgiveness, no taking away of sins. Now what has Jesus Christ done for us? He has made peace through the blood of His cross. He is the Lamb of God that taketh away the sin of the world; and the sin was what hindered peace.

Look at His precious blood shed to take away your sins! Do you see it, do you believe it? Then there is nothing between you and God, for that bleeding Hand has broken down the wall; the blood has made peace, and you may come to your heavenly Father and receive His loving forgiveness, and know that you have peace with God, through Jesus Christ our Lord.

> "Precious blood that hath redeemed us,
>   All the price is paid!
> Perfect pardon now is offered,
>   Peace is made.

> "Precious blood, whose full atonement
>   Makes us nigh to God!
> Precious blood, our song of glory,
>   Praise and laud!

> "Precious, precious blood of Jesus,
>   Ever flowing free!
> Oh believe it, oh receive it,
>   'Tis for thee!"

8.

"WHITER THAN SNOW."

"Whiter than snow."—Psalm 51:7.

BUT snow is whiter than anything else! Especially if you saw it glittering in the sunshine on the top of a high mountain, where no dust can ever reach it.   Mortal eyes have seen something as white as snow, for the raiment of the angel of the resurrection was "white as snow"; and the shining raiment of the Lord Jesus on the Mount of Transfiguration was "exceeding white as snow." But what can be made "whiter than snow"?

"Wash *me*, and *I* shall be whiter than snow!" What, *me?* my naughty, sinful self? my soul so stained with sin, that I cannot make it or keep it clean at all? Yes, "*I* shall be whiter than snow" if God washes me.

But water will not do this, and tears will not do it. Only one thing can do it, but that does it surely and thoroughly. "The blood of Jesus Christ His Son cleanseth us from all sin."

This is "the fountain opened for sin and for uncleanness"; and ever since the precious blood was shed, it has always been open. It is open now, this very evening, ready for you to be washed in it, and made "whiter than snow."

Do not stop short at thinking a little about it, but go to your heavenly Father, and ask Him to wash you in the precious blood of Christ.

Be *willing* to be *really* washed. Do not be like some little children, who do not wish to have a clean white frock put on, because they know they cannot go and play in the dirt. Be willing not to go back to the dirt any more.

And then *let* Him wash you; do not just say the words, and get up from your knees, and think no more of it; but put your very heart into His hands, and look at the precious blood of Jesus, and wait and ask Him to show you how really it was shed for you, and how really it cleanses from all sin. And then you will be ready, like the Samaritan, to fall down at Jesu's feet, "giving Him thanks" for having washed even you.

"Precious, precious blood of Jesus,
　　Let it make thee whole!
Let it flow in mighty cleansing
　　O'er thy soul.

"Though thy sins are red like crimson,
　　Deep in scarlet glow,
Jesu's precious blood can make them
　　White as snow."

9.

ASKING.

"Ask what I shall give thee."—2 Chronicles 1:7.

THERE had been a grand day in Israel. The young King Solomon had spoken to all the people, and to all the great men and captains and governors, and they had followed him to the tabernacle of the Lord, and he had gone up to the brazen altar which Bezaleel had made nearly five hundred years before, and had offered a thousand burnt-offerings. "In that night" when it was all over, and Solomon was quiet and alone, "did God appear unto Solomon, and said unto him, Ask what I shall give thee." And Solomon took God at His word, and asked at once for what he felt he wanted most. And God kept his word, and gave him at once what he asked, and promised him a great deal more besides.

This is the message to you to-night, "Ask what I shall give thee."

Think what you most want, and ask for that, for Jesus Christ's sake. You need not, like Solomon, ask for only one thing; you want many things, and you may ask for them all. And God will give—He always does give to the real askers—more than you ask, more than you ever thought of asking.

Perhaps you say, "I don't know what to ask." Then begin by asking Him to show you by His Holy Spirit what you really want, and to teach you to ask for it.

Then you say, "Will He give me whatever I ask?" Well, if you ask something which is not good for you, He loves you too much to give you that! but He will give you something better. But if you ask for something that He has promised to give, you may be quite certain He will give it you. Remind your heavenly Father of His promises, as Solomon did (2 Chronicles 1:9). And you may ask and expect the answer at once, like Solomon, who said, "*Now,* O Lord God!" and "Give me *now!*"

Then listen to God's message, and now, this very evening, ask Him for some of His promised gifts. And when you lie down, try to think of the different things which He has promised, and which you want, and turn every thought into the prayer, "Give me *now*—for Jesus Christ's sake."

> "Thou art coming to a King,
> Large petitions with thee bring;
> For His grace and power are such,
> None can ever ask too much."

10.

GOD'S BENEFITS.

"Forget not all His benefits."—Psalm 103:2.

IF some kind friend made you a present of twenty pounds to buy all sorts of things with, would you not feel rather hurt if he thought it necessary to say to you, "Do not forget that I gave you this"? Of course you would not forget, you could not possibly be so ungrateful. But what if, after all, you had forgotten, and had all your nice things around you without ever recollecting him, would it not touch your heart if he came again and said very gently, "Do not forget"?

I need not tell you Who and what I mean. You know! Have you been forgetting all His benefits, forgetting to thank Him for them, just as if they had all come of themselves? Oh, ask Him now to forgive you this sin of forgetfulness, for Jesus Christ's sake! But now that He has reminded you and forgiven you, ask Him for the Holy Spirit to help you to recollect His benefits instead of forgetting them.

"His benefits" means all the good things He has done for you, and all the good things He has given you. Try to count up "His benefits" of this one day; and then think of those of yesterday, and last week, and all the year, and all your life since you were a little baby! You will soon find that there are more than you can count, and you will begin to see how very much you have to thank Him for.

And then recollect His still greater benefits—the great gift of Jesus Christ Himself to be your Saviour and Redeemer, and the great gift of salvation through Him, and all His promises of grace and glory!

David speaks of "the multitude of His tender mercies," and Isaiah tells of "the multitude of His loving-kindnesses." Are not these true and beautiful words? Will you not turn them into a song of thanksgiving, and say, "Bless the Lord, O my soul, and forget not all his benefits: Who crowneth thee with loving-kindness and tender mercies!"

"Now my evening praise I give;
Thou didst die that I might live;
All my blessings come from Thee,
Oh how good Thou art to me!

"Thou, my best and kindest Friend,
Thou wilt love me to the end;
Let me love Thee more and more,
Always better than before."

11.

WILLING AND DOING.

"It is God which worketh in you, both to will and to do of His good
pleasure."
—Philippians 2:13.

RATHER a hard "pillow" to-night, you think! But it is what will make many hard things quite easy for you.

Have you not found it hard to be good? hard to keep from saying something naughty that you wanted to say? very hard to keep down the angry feeling, even if you did not say the angry word? hard to do a right thing, because you did not at all like doing it, and quite impossible to make yourself wish to do it? You asked God to help you to do it, and He did help you; but did you ever think of asking Him to make you *like* to do it?

Now, this is just what is meant by God's "working in you to *will*." It means that He can and will undertake the very thing which you cannot manage. He can and will "take your will, and work it for you"; making you want to do just what He wants you to do; making you like the very things that He likes, and hate just what He hates.

It is always easy to do what we like doing; so, when we have given up our will to Him, and asked Him to work it for us, it makes everything easy. For then we shall *want* to "do according to His good pleasure," and we shall be very happy in it; because trying to please Him will not be fighting against our own wills, when God has taken them and is working them for us.

Do you not see what happy days are before you if you will only take God at His word about this? Only try Him, and you will see! Tell Him that you have found you cannot manage your will yourself, and that now you will give it up to Him, and trust Him, *from now*, not only to work in you to *do,* but to work in you to *will* also, "according to His good pleasure."

> "Take my will, and make it Thine;
> It shall be no longer mine.
>
> "Take my heart, it is Thine own;
> It shall be Thy royal throne."

12.

"THOU KNOWEST"

"O Lord, Thou knowest."—Jeremiah 15:15.

THIS little text has been a comfort to many a sorrowful child, as well as to
older persons. Things are not always bright with the little ones, and they
do not always get as much sympathy as they want, because their troubles are not
exactly the same sort as those of grown-up people. Has there been something
of this kind to-day, dear little one? Have you felt troubled and downhearted,
and you could not explain it to anyone, and so no one could comfort you because no one understood? Take this little pillow to rest your tired and troubled
little heart upon to-night, "Thou knowest!" Thou, Lord Jesus, kind Shepherd
of the weary or wandering little lambs, Thou knowest all about it! Thou hast
heard the words that made me feel so sad; Thou hast seen just what happened
that troubled me; Thou knowest what I could not explain, "Thou understand-
est my thought"; Thou hast been looking down into my heart all the time, and
there is nothing hid from Thee! Thou knowest all the truth about it! and Thou
knowest all that I cannot put into words at all!

Is it not comfort already, just to know that He knows? And is it not enough
that he knows? Why, you know that He can do everything; so, surely, He can
make things come right for you (really right, not perhaps what you fancy would
be nicest and most right). And you know that He careth (that is, goes on caring)
for you; so, if He knows about your trouble, He cares about it too. And He not
only cares, but loves, so that He would not have let this trouble touch His dear
child,—when He knew about it all the time,—but that He wanted it to be a little messenger to call you to Him to be comforted, and to show you that He is
your best Friend, and to teach you the sweetness of saying, "Thou knowest!"

> "Jesus is our Shepherd
>   Wiping every tear;
> Folded in His bosom,
>   What have we to fear?
>
> "Only let us follow
>   Whither He doth lead;
> To the thirsty desert,
>   Or the dewy mead."

13.

OUR COMFORTER.

"When the Comforter is come."—John 15:26.

LITTLE children often want comforting. Something troubles you, and the grown-up people do not know, or do not think it is much to be troubled about, and so nobody comforts you, and you feel very sad. Sometimes they try, and yet it does not seem to comfort you. And sometimes you have even "refused to be comforted."

What a beautiful name this is for the Holy Spirit, "The Comforter!" so gentle, so kind, so loving. When He comes He is true to His name, and brings sweet comfort even for the little troubles of His little ones.

Is He come to you? Your heavenly Father has promised to give the Holy Spirit to them that ask Him. So, if you ask, He is sure to give. Then ask that the Holy Spirit may come into your heart, and dwell there always.

Is He come to you? Are you not quite sure whether He has come yet, or not? The rest of this verse tells you how you may know. Jesus said, "When the Comforter is come, He shall testify of me." That means, He will *tell you about Jesus*; He will put thoughts of Jesus into your mind, and love to Jesus into your heart, and He will make you see and understand more about Jesus than you did before. If you are thinking about Him, and glad to hear about Him, and trying to please Him, I think the Comforter is come, and is beginning to testify of Jesus in you.

Is He come to you? Then you will never be without a Comforter, whatever troubles come; if they are little vexations or disappointments, He can make you see the bright side, and be patient, and trustful, and happy; if they are great troubles, perhaps illness, or some dear one taken away from you, still He can so comfort you, that you will wonder and find out for the first time what a very precious gift He is, and what sweet peace can hush your sorrow "when the Comforter is come."

> "Our blest Redeemer, ere He breathed
>   His tender, last farewell,
> A Guide, a Comforter, bequeathed,
>   With us to dwell.
>
> "And His that gentle voice we hear,
>   Soft as the breath of even,
> That checks each fault, that calms each fear,
>   And speaks of heaven."

14.

THE BLIND MAN.

"What wilt thou that I shall do unto thee?"—Luke 18:41.

ONLY a blind beggar by the wayside! But Jesus of Nazareth stood still when he cried to Him. He could not grope his way among the crowd, but Jesus commanded him to be brought near to Him. He knew why the poor man had cried out, but He would have him tell it to Himself. So He said, "What wilt thou that I shall do unto thee?" Wonderful question, with a wonderful promise wrapped up in it! For it meant that the mighty Son of God was ready to do whatever this poor blind beggar asked. What did he ask? First, just what he most wanted! Not what he supposed he ought to ask, nor what anyone had taught him to ask, nor what other people asked; but simply *what he wanted*. Secondly, he asked straight off for a miracle! He never stayed to question whether it was likely or not, nor how Jesus of Nazareth would do it, nor whether it was too much to ask all at once, nor whether the people would think him too bold. He knew what he wanted, and He believed that Jesus of Nazareth could do it, and so he asked, and that was enough.

"And Jesus said unto him, Receive thy sight: thy faith hath saved thee."

And *that* was enough, his prayer of faith, and Christ's answer of power, for "immediately he received his sight." Was that all? did he go back to beg by the wayside? No; he "followed Him, glorifying God." What a change from the cry of only a few minutes before!

Just one thing more is told us in this lovely little story, "And all the people, when they saw it, gave praise unto God." See what that first cry of "Have mercy on me," so quickly led to! Who would have expected a few minutes before to have seen him with his eyes open, following Jesus, glorifying God, and causing a whole crowd to give praise to God! I think the Lord Jesus says to you to-night, "What wilt thou that I shall do unto thee?" What will you answer Him?

> "Pass me not, O tender Saviour!
> Let me love and cling to Thee;
> I am longing for Thy favour,
> When Thou comest, call for me.
> Even me."

15.

"THIS SAME JESUS."

"This same Jesus."—Acts 1:11.

"JESUS CHRIST, the same yesterday, and to-day, and forever." Yes, the very same to you to-night that He was to the disciples who stood gazing up into heaven, when, having lifted up His hands and blessed them, He went up to the opening gates of glory.

The very same to you to-night that He was to the little children, when He took them up in His arms and blessed them. Not a bit different! Just as kind, just as loving, just as ready to take you up too, and bless you, and keep you always "safe in the arms of Jesus."

The very same to you to-night that He was when He said so lovingly, "Come unto Me, all ye that labour and are heavy laden, and I will give you rest." Do you not feel that you would have loved Him ever so much if you had heard Him say that, and that you would have gone to Him at once, because He was so good and kind? Well, He is "this same Jesus" now. When you lie down, see how many sweet and gracious words and deeds of His you can recollect, and say to yourself with every one, "He is the same now, and the same for me!"

You are not always the same to Him. When He comes and knocks at the door of your heart, you are sometimes ready to open; and sometimes you give Him a cold, short, careless answer; and sometimes no answer at all. But He is always the same to you; always ready to receive you with tender love and pardon when you come to Him.

Perhaps you do not feel so happy now as you did one day when you felt that He was very near and gracious, and full of forgiving love to you? What has changed? Only your feelings, not the Lord Jesus. He is always "this same Jesus"; and you may rest on this to-night, and forever.

"For this word, O Lord, we bless Thee,
    For our Saviour's changeless name;
  Yesterday, to-day, forever,
    Jesus Christ is still the same."

16.

COME AND SEE!

"Come and see."—John 1:39, 46.

THE Lord Jesus said it first. He said it to the two disciples of John who heard that He was the Lamb of God. They knew very little about Him, but they followed Him. Perhaps they would not even have ventured to speak, but, "Jesus turned, and saw them following," and spoke to them. Then they asked Him where He dwelt, and He said, "Come and see!"

Philip said it next. He had found Christ himself, and at once he told his friend Nathanael about Him, and said, "Come and see!"

Is it not said to you to-night? Oh "come and see" Jesus! come and kneel down before Him, and look up into His glorious and loving face, and see what a lovely and precious Saviour He is! Come and see how kind and good He is! Come and see how ready He is to receive you, to take you up in His arms and bless you. Come and see what He has done for you; see how He loved you and gave Himself for you; how He lived, and suffered, and bled, and died for you! Come and see what gifts He has for you, forgiveness and peace, His Spirit and His grace, His joy and His love! Come and see where He dwelleth—see that He is ready to come in and dwell with you, to make your little heart His own dwelling-place. Oh if I could but persuade you to "come and see!" There is no other sight so glorious and beautiful. Will you not come?

When you have come, when you can say like Philip, "We have found Him!" and like St. Paul, "We see Jesus," will you not say to some one else "Come and see"? You will wish every one else to come to Him, and you have His word to bid you try to bring them: "Let him that heareth say, Come!" Will you not say "Come" to some little friend or brother or sister, or to anyone to whom He makes you wish to say it? There is no sweeter invitation for you to give than "Come and see!"

> "Jessie, if you only knew
> What He is to me,
> Surely you would love Him too,
> You would 'come and see.'
>
> "Come, and you will find it true,
> Happy you will be!
> Jesus says, and says to you,
> 'Come! Oh come to Me!'"

17.

TELLING JESUS.

"Told Him all things."—Mark 6:30.

WHEN you have been out for a day, what do you look forward to as you come home in the evening? Why do you run so eagerly into the house, and look so bright? You want to tell "all about it" to some one whom you love,—father, or mother, or brothers and sisters; and you can hardly talk fast enough to pour it all out. You begin at the beginning, and tell everything (if they will only let you stay up long enough), the pleasures and the mishaps, what has been done, or what has been said.

When each day is over, and you go up to bed, what do you tell Jesus? Do you tell Him everything too? Perhaps you do not tell Him anything at all; or perhaps you only tell Him of something that you have done wrong, and are sorry for; you never thought of such a thing as telling Him *everything*! Yet He loves you better than the dear ones down-stairs, who listened to all your little stories.

When the apostles had been away, they "gathered themselves together unto Jesus, and told Him all things, both what they had done, and what they had taught." Can you not fancy the gentle, gracious Master listening to everything so kindly, so patiently, letting them tell Him all their mistakes and all their success, all that had made them glad and all that had made them sorry? And can you not fancy the disciples sitting at His feet, and looking up into His face, and seeing how interested He was in all they had done, and not wishing to keep anything back from such a dear Master, and finding their own love to Him growing warmer and brighter for this sweet hour of talk with Him! How different if they had just said a few cold words to Him, and never *told* Him anything! Try this tonight! It will be such a help, such a comfort, and before long you will find it such a joy to tell Jesus everything!

"Tell Him all the failures,
  Tell Him all the sins;
He is kindly listening
  Till His child begins.

"Tell Him all the pleasures
  Of your merry day,
Tell Him all the treasures
  Crowning all your way."

18.

CHRIST'S DEATH FOR US.

"Our Lord Jesus Christ, who died for us."—1 Thessalonians 5:9, 10.

DIED for us? Who else ever did as much for you? who else ever loved you as much? Only think now, what it really means, because it is really true; and surely it is most horribly ungrateful, when one for whom such a great thing has been done does not even think about it.

You would think it hard to be punished for some one else's fault; but this is exactly what your dear Saviour did,—let Himself be punished for your fault instead of you.

Suppose some cruel man were going to cut off your leg, what would you think if your brother came and said, "No; chop mine off instead!" But that would not be dying for you. And "our Lord Jesus Christ *died*" for you.

It was the very most He could do, to show His exceeding great love to you. He was not obliged to go through with it; He might have come down from the cross any moment. The nails could not have kept Him there an instant longer than He chose; His love and pity were the real nails that nailed Him fast to the cross till the very end, till He could say, "It is finished," till He "*died* for us."

It was not only because He loved His Father that He did it, but because He loved us; for the text goes on—"Who died for us, that, whether we wake or sleep, we might live together with Him." So He loved us so much that He wanted us to live together with Him; and as no sin can enter His holy and beautiful home, He knew our sins must be taken away before we could go there. And only blood could take away sin, only death could atone for it; and so He bled, that we might be washed in His most precious blood; He died, "that, whether we wake or sleep, we might live together with Him."

> "There is a word I fain would speak,
>   Jesus died!
> O eyes that weep, and hearts that break,
>   Jesus died!
> No music from the quivering string
> Could such sweet sounds of rapture bring;
> O may I always love to sing,
>   Jesus died! Jesus died!"

19.

NOTHING, OR EVERYTHING?

"Is it nothing to you?"—Lamentations 1:12.

THIS was said of a great, great sorrow, which should have touched the heart of every one who passed by and saw it, the terrible troubles that came upon Jerusalem and her children. But this was also a type of the far more terrible cup of sorrow which the Lord Jesus drank for us, drank it willingly, so that we might drink of the river of His pleasures. Listen! for it is as if He said to you and me, "Is it nothing to you, all ye that pass by? behold and see if there be any sorrow like unto my sorrow!"

"Behold and see" how all His life He was "a Man of sorrows," not having where to lay His head; His own brethren refusing to believe in Him, the wicked Jews hating Him, and over and over again trying to kill Him, and He knowing all the while what awful suffering was before Him.

"Behold and see" Him in the garden of Gethsemane, "being in an agony," and saying, "My soul is exceeding sorrowful, even unto death."

"Behold and see" Him, scourged and spit upon, led as a lamb to the slaughter, and then nailed to the cross; suffering even unto death, thirsting in the terrible pain, and yet not drinking to still it, and saying in the midst of it all, "My God, my God, why hast Thou forsaken me?" Was ever any sorrow like unto the sorrow that our Lord Jesus Christ went through for love of us? Is it nothing to you? Can you look at it and not care about it? Can you "pass by" and go on just the same as if He had never loved and suffered?

Oh, instead of "nothing," let it be henceforth *everything* to you! Let it be the reason why you hate sin and why you try to do right; let it be your peace and joy, your strength and your song; let it fill your heart with love and gratitude; let it make you brave and determined to live for Him who suffered and died for you.

"See, oh see, what love the Saviour
    Also hath on us bestowed;
How He bled for us and suffered,
    How He bare the heavy load.
On the cross and in the garden
    Oh how sore was His distress!
Is not this a love that passeth
    Aught that tongue can e'er express?"

20.

THE BEAUTY OF THE LORD JESUS.

"Yea, He is altogether lovely."—Song of Solomon 5:16.

H E! We do not need to ask "Who?" for these words could only be said of One—the Beloved One, the Holy One, the Blessed One, the Glorious One! Only of Jesus, *our* Lord Jesus, whom having not seen we love, whom we shall see one day in all His beauty, "when He shall come to be glorified in His saints, and to be admired in all them that believe!" Oh if we could see Him now, as He is at this very moment, sitting at the right hand of the Majesty on high, Himself the very brightness of God's glory, the splendour would be too great, we should fall at His feet as dead, as St. John did, unless He strengthened us to behold His glory. But if He laid His right hand upon us, saying, "Fear not," and we looked again, what should we see? Oh what loveliness! oh what unspeakable beauty! "Fairer than the children of men," and "the chiefest among ten thousand," is our Lord Jesus! And in all the glory He is "this same Jesus"; although His countenance is now as the sun shineth in his strength, there is the gentle smile for His little children, and the tender kindness for the sick ones, and the wonderful, wonderful look of mighty love that would bring the whole world to His feet if they could only see it. And there are scars too, which make His very beauty more beautiful, for they are scars of love. He did not lose the print of the nails when He rose from the grave, and the angels and redeemed ones around Him can see them even now; for even "in the midst of the throne" He is the "Lamb, as it had been slain." So the love has overflowed the glory, and our Lord Jesus is "altogether lovely." Our Lord Jesus! Yes, for the Altogether Lovely One has given Himself for us, and given Himself to us; so that even the least of His little ones may look up and say, "This is my Beloved, and this is my Friend!"

> "Oh Saviour, precious Saviour,
>   My heart is at Thy feet;
> I bless Thee, and I love Thee,
>   And Thee I long to meet.
>
> "To see Thee in Thy beauty,
>   To see Thee face to face,
> To see Thee in Thy glory,
>   And reap Thy smile of grace!"

21.

THE COMING OF THE LORD JESUS.

"Behold, He cometh!"—Revelation 1:7.

DOES this seem a terrible verse? do you wonder why it should be one of the "little pillows," and wish the book had given you a different one to go to sleep upon to-night? Look at it again: "He cometh!" Who? Jesus Himself, the "same Jesus" who said, "Come unto Me." You thought it would be so nice to come, if you could only see Him. But you will see Him, for He is coming.

Think of seeing Him come, so beautiful, so glorious, so "altogether lovely"; Him, the very same dear, kind Saviour, who loves the little children, who loves you and has called you! Seeing His very face; the very brow that was crowned with thorns, the very eyes that looked on Peter, the very lips that said such wonderful and gracious things! No longer thinking about Him, and trying to believe on Him and praying to Him, and wishing for Him, but really seeing Him! Is *this* terrible? Does it not rather seem something to look forward to very much?

Only one thing would make it terrible, and that is, if you will not come to Him now, and will not let Him wash away your sins in His precious blood. Then it would indeed be terrible, for He would never any more say to you "Come!" but only "Depart!"

But you want Him to wash you clean, do you not? and you did try to come to Him? And you believe He means what He says, and really died to save you? Then, oh! shall you not be glad to see Him? What if now the cry were heard, "Jesus is coming!" Your heart would beat quick, but I think it would be with gladness, not with terror. Jesus is coming! Would you not go forth to meet Him? Jesus is coming! Could anything be happier news? I think we shall not think much about the sound of the trumpet, and the clouds of glory, and all the holy angels that come with Him; we shall "see Jesus," and hear His own voice, and that will fill our eyes and our hearts forever.

"Thou art coming, O my Saviour!
Thou art coming. O my King!
In Thy beauty all-resplendent,
In Thy glory all-transcendent,
Well may we rejoice and sing!"

22.

MY KING!

"Now then do it."—2 Samuel 3:18.

DAVID had been anointed king over Israel long before, but the people did not own him while Saul was their king. Then after long wars and troubles Saul was killed. But still it was only Judah who followed David; and for seven years and a half Israel held back. At last Abner said to the elders of Israel, "Ye sought in times past for David to be king over you, *Now then do it!*" And they did it.

Now God has long ago anointed the Lord Jesus to be our King, but is He your own king yet? is He reigning in your heart? Have you ever come to Him and said, "Thou shalt be *my* King, Lord Jesus"?

Perhaps, like the Israelites, you have "sought in times past for Him to be King over you"; you have been wishing He would come and reign, and put down all the wrong tempers and naughty thoughts which master you sometimes like strong rebels. Do you really wish it? Then that wish is like a messenger sent to prepare the way before Him; but wishing is not enough—"Now then *do* it!" Now, this very night, before you go to sleep, tell the dear Saviour, who has been waiting, to come and set up His kingdom of peace and joy in your heart, that He shall be your King *now!* Own Him your King at once; say to Him reverently, and lovingly, and with all your heart, "Jesus, my King!"

Then, when Satan tries to get back to his old throne in your heart, tell him it cannot be his ever again, for you have given it up to your King Jesus, and that He is to reign there always now; and that He will not give it up, but will fight for you, and put down all the rebels.

Do not say, "Oh yes, I should like this very much!" and just go to sleep as usual; but "now then *do* it!" and then lie down with the happy thought, "My King!"

> "Reign over me, Lord Jesus!
>   Oh make my heart Thy throne!
> It shall be Thine, dear Saviour,
>   It shall be Thine alone.
>
> "Oh come and reign, Lord Jesus;
>   Rule over everything!
> And keep me always loyal,
>   And true to Thee, my King!"

23.

CALLED BY NAME.

"I have called thee by thy name."—Isaiah 43:1.

LOOK out, if it is a clear night, and see the stars sparkling all over the sky. You cannot count them; no one can, because there are more than eyes or telescopes have ever reached. But "He calleth them all by names," knows every one separately. And yet, though He has all those wonderful worlds of light in His hands, and "bringeth out their host by number," He turns to say to each of His poor little weak children on this dark earth, "I have called thee by thy name." He knows your name; you are not merely one of the rest to Him, you are _____ to Him. Take a pencil and write your own name there, it will be perfectly true!

That name was given you in His presence, and by His minister, when you were baptized, in obedience to our Saviour's command; that very name is a token that you are called to be His own child. God knows it, and calls you by it.

But He has done more than this. Why do you care to read this little book every night? why do you care to hear about the things which are "not seen,"—about Jesus, and salvation, and heaven? What is it that seems like a little voice within, persuading you to seek and love Jesus? That is God's own voice in your heart, calling you by name! For you know it is to *you*, because it is only in your own heart; no one else hears it, no one else even knows of it. When He calls thus, listen, and see what else He has to say to you: "Fear not; for I have redeemed thee, I have called thee by thy name; thou art mine!"

"Jesus is our Shepherd,
    For the sheep He bled;
Every lamb is sprinkled
    With the blood He shed.

"Then on each He setteth
    His own secret sign;
'They that have My Spirit,
    These,' saith He, 'are mine.'"

24.

MY JEWELS.

"That day when I make up my jewels."—Malachi 3:17.

" M Y jewels!" God tells us who they are—"Every one that feared the Lord, and that thought upon His name." Then if you fear the Lord, and think upon His name, you are one of His jewels, and all that you are going to read about them is for you, and means *you*.

"My jewels!" They are His "special treasure" (see margin), His very own, dearer than all other treasures to Him. We see how very precious they are to Him by the price He paid for them. For every one of them has been purchased, not with silver and gold (all the silver and gold in the world would not have been enough to purchase one of them), but with the precious blood of Christ. That was the greatest thing God had to give, and He gave it for them.

God has found and chosen His jewels, and He will never lose them. Every one of them is kept safe in the casket of His everlasting love. He does not mean to hide them away, and be ashamed of them; for He says they shall "be a crown of glory in the hand of the Lord, and a royal diadem in the hand of thy God." They are not all the same, jewels are of many different colours and sizes; but the day is coming when He will make them up,—when they will all be gathered together in His treasury, and shine together in His glorious crown, and not one will be forgotten, or overlooked, or lost, for every one is "precious in His sight."

Is it not a grand thing to be one of God's jewels? How very wonderful that He should give such a beautiful name to His poor, sinful, worthless children, and set such shining hopes before them! Ought we not to try to walk worthy of this high and holy calling?

> "Sons of Zion, ye are precious
>   In your heavenly Father's sight;
> Ye are His peculiar treasure,
>   And His jewels of delight.
>
> "Sought and chosen, cleansed and polished,
>   Purchased with transcendent cost,
> Kept in His own royal casket,
>   Never, never to be lost."

25.

ALWAYS MORE!

"He giveth more grace."—James 4:6.

YES, always more! And if He has given any at all, it is a certain proof that He will give more; for over and over again the Lord Jesus said, "Whosoever hath, to him shall be given." So, if He has given you a little grace, just enough to wish for more, you shall have more; and then when He has given you more, that will be the very reason why you may expect more still. Is it not nice to be always looking forward to "grace for grace"?

Then, as you grow older, and the little vessel grows larger, He will keep on pouring more grace into it. You will outgrow many things, but you will never outgrow this rich and precious supply.

"He giveth more grace" than we ask. If He had given us only what we asked, we should never have had any at all, for it is His grace that first of all makes us wish, and teaches us to ask for it. And He says, "Open thy mouth wide, and I will fill it." Then open it wide! ask Him to fill you with His grace.

"He giveth more grace" than all our need. It never runs short. Whatever our need is, there is quite enough grace for it, and then "more" too! *always* more. If our need seems to become greater, we shall find the grace greater too, if we will but go to Him who giveth it; if the enemies that we are trying to fight against seem stronger than ever, we shall certainly find His grace stronger too, if we will only ask it, and take it, and use it.

We can never overtake this promise, much less outrun it; for however little we have, or however much we want, now this moment, and on to the end of our lives, it is always, always, "He giveth *more* grace!"

> "Have you on the Lord believed?
> Still there's more to follow;
> Of His grace have you received?
> Still there's more to follow.
> Oh the grace the Father shows!
> Still there's more to follow;
> Freely He His grace bestows,
> Still there's more to follow.
>
> "More and more! more and more!
> Always more to follow!
> Oh His matchless, boundless love!
> Still there's more to follow!"

26.

SATISFIED.

"Shall never thirst."—John 4:14.

WHEN you have had a treat or a pleasure, do not you begin to wish for another? When you look over your playthings or your books (whichever you happen to care most for), have you not said, "If I only had just this, or just that besides"? And even some favoured little ones who hardly know what to wish for, because they seem to have everything, have not enough to make them *quite* happy; they want something, without knowing what they want. Is not this something like feeling thirsty?

And when you get the very thing you most wanted, it does not make much difference, for you very soon want something else; you are "thirsty" again.

The Lord Jesus knows all about this, and so He said, "Whosoever drinketh of this water, shall thirst again; but whosoever drinketh of the water that I shall give him, shall never thirst." First, you see you are quite sure to "thirst again"; it is no use expecting to find anything earthly that will satisfy you. Secondly, Jesus has something to give you which will make you *quite* satisfied and glad. Thirdly, as long as you go on drinking this, you will be *always* satisfied and glad. Fourthly, you cannot get it from any one or anything else. Jesus gives it, and Jesus only. Fifthly, it must be meant for you, because He says "whosoever," and that means "anybody that likes!" And He says, "Ho, every one that thirsteth, come ye to the waters!" And, "If any man thirst, let him come unto me and drink." And, "I will give unto him that is athirst of the fountain of the water of life freely."

Will you not say to Him, like the poor woman at the well, "Lord Jesus, give me this water, that I thirst not!" Listen to his kind answer! "Drink, yea, drink abundantly, O beloved!"

> "I heard the voice of Jesus say,
>   Behold, I freely give
> The living water; thirsty one,
>   Stoop down, and drink, and live.
>
> "I came to Jesus, and I drank
>   Of that life-giving stream;
> My thirst was quenched, my soul revived,
>   And now I live in him."

27.

OUR SURETY.

"I will be surety for him."—Genesis 43:9.

JUDAH, the elder brother, promised his father to bring Benjamin safely back from Egypt. He undertook this entirely. He said, "I will be surety for him; of my hand shalt thou require him: if I bring him not unto thee, and set him before thee, then let me bear the blame forever." And his father trusted Judah to do as he had said, and so Judah was surety for Benjamin.

Jesus Christ is Surety for us. He, our Elder Brother, undertakes to bring us safely to the house of His Father and our Father. He undertakes to present us before the presence of His glory. We are in His hand, and from His hand God will require us and receive us. And God, who so loves His children, has trusted the Lord Jesus to do this. He has given us to Him, and He has accepted Jesus Christ as our Surety.

Now, if God has trusted Him, will not you trust Him too? What! hesitate about trusting Jesus? Whom else could you trust? Who else could undertake to bring you safe to heaven? Benjamin might possibly have found his way by himself from Egypt to Canaan; but never, never could you find the way by yourself from earth to heaven; and never, never could anyone but the Lord Jesus bring you there.

Benjamin could not be quite certain that his brother could keep his promise, for Judah was only a man, and might have been killed in Egypt. But you may be quite certain that your Elder Brother *can* keep His promise, for He is God as well as man. And do you think He *would* break His promise? He, the Faithful Saviour, break His promise? Heaven and earth shall pass away, but His word shall not pass away!

Then trust Him now, and never wrong His faithful love again by leaving off trusting Him. He is our Surety, and He will bring every one who trusts Him safe to the heavenly Canaan.

> "Jesus, I will trust Thee, trust Thee with my soul!
> Guilty, lost, and helpless, Thou canst make me whole!
> Jesus, I do trust Thee, trust without a doubt!
> 'Whosoever cometh, Thou wilt not cast out.'"

28.

OUR FORERUNNER.

"He shall go over before."—Deuteronomy 3:28.

JOSHUA was a type of Christ in many things. God gave him to be "a leader and commander of the people." He was their captain in war, and their saviour from their enemies.

In this verse God told Moses that Joshua should go over before the people into Canaan, and "cause them to inherit the land."

This is what the Lord Jesus Christ has done for us. He has gone before, in front of, the great army of the living God who have crossed or have yet to cross the river of death. His blessed feet have passed that river, and made the crossing easy for us, so that the dark waters shall never overflow one of us, not even a little child.

He has gone before us into the beautiful land to prepare the many mansions for us. He is there, waiting for us, ready to give us His own most sweet and gracious welcome to His own fair country, as soon as our feet have crossed the river.

Will you fear to go where Jesus has gone before? Will you fear to go where He is? You know you must die. You know that even little children die who are much younger than you. And very likely you do not like to think about dying. I do not think you need think at all about lying cold and dead and being put in the grave. When that does come, it will not matter to you in the least. If Jesus is your Saviour, if He takes away your sins, death will only be like being carried in a minute across a narrow stream, and meeting the loving and glorious One on the other side, where He is gone over before. Nay, rather, He will come and fetch you Himself into the "pleasant land," and He will "cause you to inherit" it, so that it will be your own land, your own beautiful and holy and glorious home forever.

> "Praying for His children,
>   In that blessèd place,
> Calling them to glory,
>   Sending them His grace;
>
> "His bright home preparing,
>   Little ones, for you;
> Jesus ever liveth,
>   Ever loveth too."

29.

" PLEASURES FOR EVERMORE."

"At Thy right hand there are pleasures for evermore."—Psalm 16:11.

YOU never had a pleasure that lasted. You look forward to a great pleasure, and it comes, and then very soon it is gone, and you can only look back upon it. The very longest and pleasantest day you ever had came to an end, and you had to go to bed and know that it was over.

How different are the pleasures at God's right hand! They are for evermore, and you cannot get to the end or see to the end of " evermore," for there is no end to it.

And you see it is not one pleasure only, but "*pleasures*," as manifold as they are unending. Do you not wonder what they will be? We cannot even guess at most of them; and if we thought and imagined the brightest and best that we possibly could, we should still find, when we reached heaven, that God's " pleasures " for us were ever so much greater and better than we thought.

We can tell a few things about them. They will be holy pleasures, never mingled with any sin. They will be perfect pleasures, with nothing whatever to spoil them. They will be lasting pleasures, for to-night's text says so. They will be abundant pleasures, as many as we can possibly wish, for David says (Psalm 36:8), "They shall be *abundantly satisfied* with the fatness of Thy house, and Thou shalt make them drink of the river of Thy pleasures." They will be always freshly-flowing pleasures, for they are a river, not a little pool. They will be pleasures given by God Himself to us, for it does not say " they shall drink," but "*Thou* shalt *make them* drink of the river of *Thy* pleasures."

And all these " God hath prepared " for you. Is He not good and kind?

> " Angel voices sweetly singing,
> Echoes through the blue dome ringing,
> News of wondrous gladness bringing,
>   Ah, 'tis heaven at last!

> " Not a tear-drop ever falleth,
> Not a pleasure ever palleth,
> Song to song forever calleth;
>   Ah, 'tis heaven at last!"

30.

THE GREAT PROMISE.

"This is the promise that He hath promised us, even eternal life."—1 John 2:25.

A S the gift of the Holy Spirit was specially "the promise of the Father," so it seems that the gift of eternal life was specially the promise of the Lord Jesus. If you look in the Gospel of St. John, you will find that He promised it not only once or twice, but fifteen times! So no wonder St. John in his Epistle calls it "*the* promise which He hath promised us."

If you made me a promise, even if you said it only once, you would expect me to believe it, would you not? And you would be vexed and hurt if I would not believe it. It would seem as if I thought you were not speaking the truth. And suppose I did not say whether I believed it or not, but simply took no notice at all of what you said, would not that be quite as bad?

Now when the Lord Jesus Himself has made us a great promise, does He not expect us to believe it? Surely it grieves Him more than anything when we will not believe His kind words. And it seems almost worse when we do not take any notice of them, but go on just the same as if He had never promised anything at all.

So you see it is not only that you *may* believe this great promise of the Lord Jesus, but that you *ought* to believe it, and that you are wronging His love and grieving His heart as long as you do not believe it.

No matter that you do not deserve it; that is true enough! but He has promised it!

No matter that it seems "too good to be true"; for He has promised it! No matter that you don't feel as if you had got it yet,—He has promised it!

Only ask Him to give you faith like Abraham's, who was "fully persuaded that what He had promised He was able also to perform," so that you may say joyfully, "This is the promise that He hath promised *me*, even eternal life!"

> "Life alone is found in Jesus,
> Only there 'tis offered thee,
> Offered without price or money,
> 'Tis the gift of God sent free.
> Take salvation!
> Take it now and happy be!"

31.

CERTAINTY.

"Hath He said, and shall He not do it?"—Numbers 23:19.

WE have been thinking, night after night, of some of our Father's promises, and very likely you have been hoping and wishing that they would come true for you. But being quite sure is better and happier than hoping and wishing, is it not? Now, how may you be quite sure that all these "exceeding great and precious promises" will come true for you? Just simply because God has spoken them! and "hath He *said*, and shall He not do it?" Of course He will! Surely that is enough!

If your father had promised to give you a great treat, would you go about in a dismal way, saying, "Yes, it would be very nice? I hope papa will do it!" Would he be pleased at that? But if you came again, and reminded him of his promise, and he answered, "I have said it, and do you suppose I shall not do it?" what a silly child you would be if you still looked dismal, and went on only "hoping" he might do it! And what an ungrateful and unbelieving child you would be if you did not say brightly, "Thank you, dear papa!" and show him how glad you were about it, and try your very best to be good and please him all day, because he had made you such a kind and sure promise!

When you read the Bible, or hear it read, keep looking out for God's promises. They are scattered all over the Bible, like beautiful bright stars. Then, every time you come to one of them, say to yourself, This will come true for me, for "hath He said, and shall He not do it?"

Before you go to sleep, see if you can recollect as many promises as you are years old, and set upon every one this strong and shining seal, "Hath He said, and shall He not do it?"

When you reach the heavenly Canaan, you will find, as Joshua said, that "Not one thing hath failed of all the good things which the Lord your God spake concerning you; all are come to pass unto you, and not one thing hath failed thereof."—Joshua 23:14.

> "All that He hath spoken,
> He will surely do!
> Nothing shall be broken,
> Every word is true."

Sketty Schools.
Aug 14.

F.R.H. drew this on August 14, 1854, when she was 17. Sketty is next to Swansea, the city on the southern coast of Wales.

MORNING BELLS;

OR,

WAKING THOUGHTS FOR THE LITTLE ONES.

BY

FRANCES RIDLEY HAVERGAL.

TO

THE TWIN BROTHERS,

WILLIE AND ETHELBERT,

WITH

AUNT FANNY'S LOVE.

CONTENTS.

MORNING BELLS.

M OST of the readers of this little book will have already read
      Little Pillows. Those were given you to go to sleep upon night
after night; sweet, soothing texts, that little hearts might rest upon.

But in the morning we want something to arouse us, and to help
us to go brightly and bravely through the day. So here are "Morning
Bells" to waken up the little hearts, and to remind them that we must
not only rest in Jesus, but walk in Him. If the motto of "Little Pillows"
might be "Come to Jesus," the motto of "Morning Bells" might be
"Follow Jesus."

May He who loves the little ones bless this tiny effort to help them
follow Him day by day.

Wayside Chimes. May.

Love for love.

"We have known & believed the love that God hath to us." I John 4.16

Knowing that the God on high,
    With a tender Father's grace,
Waits to hear your faintest cry,
    Waits to show a Father's face, —
Stay & think! oh should not you
Love this gracious Father too?

Knowing Christ was crucified,
    Knowing that He loves you now
Just as much as when He died
    With the thorns upon His brow, —
Stay & think! oh should not you
Love this blessed Saviour too?

Knowing that the Spirit strives
    With your weary, wandering heart,
Who would change the restless lives,
    Pure & perfect peace impart, —
Stay & think! oh should not you
Love this loving Spirit too?

Frances Ridley Havergal

A fair copy autograph of "Love for Love" by F.R.H., written February 12, 1879. See page vi.

1.

CHRIST'S CHILDHOOD.

"Thy holy child Jesus."—Acts 4:30.

I F I asked, "How old are you?" you would give an exact answer. "Eight and
a half"; "Just turned ten"; "Eleven next month." Now you have thought
of God's "holy child Jesus" as a little baby, and as twelve years old in the temple, but did you ever think of Him as being *exactly* your own age? that He was
once really just as old as you are this very day? He knows what it is to be eight,
and nine, and ten years old, or whatever you may be. God's word has only told
us this one thing about those years, that He was a *holy* child.

What is "holy"? It is everything that is perfectly beautiful and good and
lovable, without anything to spoil it. This is just what He was when He was
your age. He was gentle and brave, and considerate and unselfish, noble and
truthful, obedient and loving, kind and forgiving,—everything you can think
of that you ever admired or loved in anyone else was all found together in Him,
and all this not only outside but inside, for He was "holy."

Why did He live all these holy child-years on earth instead of staying in
heaven till it was time to come and die for you? One reason was, that He might
leave you a beautiful example, so that you might wish to be like Him, and ask
for the Holy Spirit to make you like Him. But the other was even more gracious and wonderful, it was "that we might be made the righteousness of God
in Him." That is, that all this goodness and holiness might be reckoned to you,
because you had not any of your own, and that God might smile on you *for His
sake*, just as if *you* had been perfectly obedient, and truthful, and unselfish, and
good, and give you Jesus Christ's reward, which you never deserved at all, but
which He deserved for you.

He took your sins and gives you His righteousness; He took your punishment and gives you His reward; it is just changed over, if you will only accept
the exchange!

> "I'm glad my blessèd Saviour
> Was once a child like me,
> To show how pure and holy
> His little ones might be.
> And if I try to follow
> His footsteps here below,
> He never will forget me,
> Because He loves me so."

2.

OUR GREAT EXAMPLE.

"Even Christ pleased not Himself."—Romans 15:3.

D O you really wish to follow the footsteps of the Holy Child Jesus? Have you asked God to make you more like Him? Are you ready to begin to-day? Then here is a motto for to-day: "Even Christ pleased not Himself." Will you take it, and try to imitate Him? You are sure to have plenty of opportunities of acting upon it, and thus proving not only to others, but to your dear Saviour Himself, that you mean what you say, and mean what you pray.

Perhaps it seems a rather melancholy "morning bell" to you, tolling instead of chiming! But if you really wish to be like Christ, you will soon find that its music is as sweet as any, and that its quiet chime will come to you again and again with a wonderful sweetness and power, helping you over all sorts of difficulties, and saving you from all sorts of sins and troubles.

You cannot tell, till you have fairly tried, how happy a little girl can feel, who has cheerfully given up to another, for Jesus' sake, something which she would have liked for herself; nor how happy a boy can be when of his own free will, and by God's grace, he has chosen to do what his conscience tells him would please the Lord Jesus instead of what would have pleased himself.

If you have never tried it yet, begin to-day, and you will find it is quite a new happiness.

Ah, what would have become of us if Christ had only "pleased Himself," and had stayed in His own glorious home instead of coming down to save us! Think of that when you are tempted to please yourself instead of pleasing Him, and the remembrance that even He pleased not Himself because He so loved you, will help you to try and please Him and to please others for His sake.

> "If washed in Jesus' blood,
>   Then bear His likeness too!
> And as you onward press,
>   Ask,'What would Jesus do?'
>
> "Give with a full, free hand;
>   God freely gives to you!
> And check each selfish thought
>   With,'What would Jesus do?'"

3.

UPHOLDING.

"Hold Thou me up, and I shall be safe."—Psalm 119:117.

THE path is not easy. There are rough stones over which we may stumble, if we are not walking very carefully. There are places which look quite smooth, but they are more dangerous than the rough ones, for they are slippery. There are little holes hidden under flowers, which may catch our feet and give us a bad fall. There are muddy ditches, into which we may slip and get sadly wet and dirty.

How are we to walk safely along such a path? We want a strong, kind hand to hold us up, and to hold us always; a hand that will hold ours so tightly and lovingly, that it will be as the old Scotchwoman said, "Not my grip of Christ, but Christ's grip of me!" Yes, Christ's loving hand is "able to keep you from falling"; only "let your hand be restfully in the hand of Jesus," and "then shalt thou walk in thy way safely, and thy foot shall not stumble."

But do not spoil the chime of this morning's bells by ringing only half a peal! Do not say, "Hold thou me up," and stop there, or add, "But, all the same, I shall stumble and fall!" Finish the peal with God's own music, the bright words of faith that He puts into your mouth, "Hold thou me up, *and I shall be safe!*" So you will if you do not distrust Him, if you will but *trust* Him to do just what you ask, and let Him hold you up.

It would be hard to find a prayer in the Bible without a promise to match it; so David says, "Uphold me, according to Thy word."

What has He said about it? More than there is room for on this page. "I the Lord thy God will hold thy right hand." "Yea, I will uphold thee." "He will not suffer thy foot to be moved." "When thou runnest thou shalt not stumble." "Yea, he shall be holden up." "He shall keep thy foot from being taken." "He will keep the feet of His saints." Seven promises in answer to your one little prayer!

"I the Lord am with thee,
　Be thou not afraid!
I will help and strengthen,
　Be thou not dismayed!
Yea, I will uphold thee
　With My own right hand;
Thou art called and chosen
　In My sight to stand."

4.

WHAT CAN I DO?

"Bear ye one another's burdens, and so fulfil the law of Christ."—Galatians 6:2.

PERHAPS you never thought that anyone around you had any! Then if you want to fulfil this law of Christ, the first thing will be to find out who has any burdens, and which of them you could bear instead. You will not have to watch long! There are very few without any. Little backs cannot bear great burdens, but sometimes those who have great burdens have little ones too, and it makes such a difference if some loving little hand will take one or two of these. If your mother was carrying a great heavy parcel, would it not help her if you took two or three little ones out of her hand and carried them for her? So perhaps she has troubles that you do not even know about, and you see she looks tired and anxious. And it tires her a little more, because a little brother or sister wants to be nursed or amused. Now if you put your own affairs by, and call the little ones away, and amuse them quietly so that mamma may not be disturbed, this is bearing one of her burdens. Never mind if it is really a little burden to you too; is it not worth it, when it is fulfilling the law of Christ? If for a moment a burden that you have taken up does seem rather hard, and you are tempted to drop it again, think of what the Lord Jesus bore for you! Think how He took up the heaviest burden of all for you, when He "His own self bore our sins in His own body on the tree!" He did not drop that burden, but bore it till He died under it. Think of that, and it will be easy then to bear something for His sake.

Now be on the watch all to-day for little burdens to bear for others. See how many you can find out, and pick up, and carry away! Depend upon it, you will not only make it a brighter day for others, but for yourself too!

> "Little deeds of kindness,
> Little words of love,
> Make our earth an Eden,
> Like the heaven above."

5.

INSTRUMENTS.

"Yield ... your members as instruments of righteousness unto God."—Romans 6:13.

THIS does not sound so easy and tuneful as most of your other "morning bells," you think! But listen for a few minutes and you will hear the music.

What are your members? Hands, feet, lips, eyes, ears, and so on. What are you to do with them? "Yield" them, that is, give them up altogether, hand them over to God.

What for? That He may use them as instruments of righteousness. That is, just as we should take an instrument of music, to make music with it, so He may take your hands and feet and all your members, and use them to do right and good things with.

If a little one gives himself or herself to God, every part of that little body is to be God's little servant, a little instrument for Him to use.

The little hands will no longer serve Satan by striking or pinching; the little feet will not kick or stamp, nor drag and dawdle, when they ought to run briskly on some errand; the little lips will not pout; the little tongue will not move to say a naughty thing. All the little members will leave off serving Satan, and find something to do for God; for if you "yield" them to God, He will really take them and use them.

He will tell the hands to pick up what a tired mamma has dropped, and to fetch her a footstool; and the fingers to sew patiently at a warm petticoat for a poor child, or to make warm cuffs for a poor old man. He will tell the feet to run on errands of kindness and help. He will set the lips to sing happy hymns, which will cheer and comfort somebody, even if you never know of it. He will use the eyes for reading to some poor sick or blind woman, or to some fretful little one in your own home. You will be quite surprised to find in how many ways He will really use even your little members, if you give them and your whole self to Him. It will be so nice! You will never be miserable again with "nothing to do!"

> "Take my hands, and let them move
> At the impulse of Thy love.
> Take my feet, and let them be
> Swift and 'beautiful' for Thee."

6.

WILLING AND GLAD.

"Then the people rejoiced, for that they offered willingly."—1 Chronicles
29:9.

WE thought yesterday morning about giving our members up to God for
Him to use. Did you think you would like to give them up to Him?
did you yield them to Him? If you did, you will understand this morning's
text! David the king asked his people to help in bringing offerings for God's
house and service. He said, "Who then is willing to consecrate his service this
day unto the Lord?" And God made them all willing to bring what they could.
And what then? "Then the people rejoiced, for that they offered willingly, because with perfect heart they offered willingly to the Lord." "And did eat and
drink on that day before the Lord with great gladness."

See what came of offering willingly to the Lord—they "rejoiced," and everything they did, even eating and drinking, was "with great gladness." Never is anyone so happy as those who offer their own selves willingly to the Lord.
He gives them a thousandfold return for the worthless little self and weak little
members which they have offered to Him. He gives them peace, and gladness,
and blessing, beyond what they ever expected to have.

But this was not all; it was not only the people who had such a glad day, but
"David the king also rejoiced with great joy." Those who loved their king, and
recollected how much sorrow he had gone through, and how many battles he
had fought for them, must have been glad indeed to see Him rejoicing because
they had offered willingly. And I think our King, *your* King Jesus, rejoices over
us when He has made us able (1 Chronicles 29:14) to offer ourselves willingly
to Him. Is not this best of all? Jesus, who suffered for us, and who fought the
great battle of our salvation for us, He, our own beloved King, "will rejoice over
thee with joy; He will rest in His love; He will joy over thee with singing."

> "In full and glad surrender I give myself to Thee,
> Thine utterly, and only, and evermore to be!
> O Son of God, who lovest me, I will be Thine alone;
> And all I have, and all I am, shall henceforth be Thine own."

7.

FAITHFULNESS.

"Faithful over a few things."—Matthew 25:21, 23.

THE servant who had only two talents to trade with, but traded faithfully with them, had just the same glorious words spoken to him as the servant who had five talents: "Well done, good and faithful servant: thou hast been faithful over a few things ... enter thou into the joy of thy lord." Think what it would be to hear the Lord Jesus saying that to you, really to you! Oh how sweet! how blessed! how you would listen to that gracious voice saying those wonderfully gracious words to *you!*

But could He say them to you? Are you "faithful over a few things"? He has given every one, even the youngest, a few things to be faithful over, and so He has to you. Your "few things" may be very few, and very small things, but He expects you to be faithful over them.

What is being faithful over them? It means doing the very best you can with them; doing as much for Jesus as you can with your money, even if you have very little; doing as much for Him as you can with your time; doing whatever duties He gives you as well as ever you can,—your lessons, your work, the little things that you are bidden or asked to do every day, the little things that you have promised or undertaken to do for others. It means doing all these just the same whether others see you or know about it or not.

You sigh over all this; you recollect many things in which you have not been quite faithful; you know you do not deserve for Him to call you "good and faithful servant." But come at once to your gracious Lord, and ask Him to forgive all the unfaithfulness, and to make you faithful to-day. And then, even if it is only a matter of a French verb or a Latin noun, you will find it a help to recollect, "Faithful over a few things!"

"Only, O Lord, in Thy dear love,
Fit us for perfect rest above;
And help us, this and every day,
To live more nearly as we pray."

8.

"ON MINE ACCOUNT."

"Put that on mine account."—Philemon 18.

WHEN St. Paul asked Philemon, in a most beautiful letter, to take back Onesimus, who had run away from him, he said, "If he hath wronged thee, or oweth thee ought, put that on my account." Onesimus had been a bad servant to Philemon; and being willing to come back and do better, would not pay for what he had wronged him in before, and would not pay his old debts. And he evidently had nothing himself to pay them with. But St. Paul offered to pay all, so that Onesimus might be received, "not now as a servant," but as a "brother beloved."

This is an exquisite picture of what the Lord Jesus Christ does. He not only intercedes for us with Him from whom we have departed, and against whom we have sinned; but, knowing to the full how much we have wronged God, and how much we owe Him, He says, "Put that on mine account."

And God has put it all on His account, and the account has been paid, paid in blood. When "the Lord laid on Him the iniquity of us all," Jesus saw and knew all your sins; and He said, "Put that on mine account."

Oh what wonderful "kindness and love of God our Saviour"! Let the remembrance of it be like a silver bell, ringing softly and clearly whenever you are going to do, or letting yourself feel or think, something that is not right.

"Put *that* on mine account!" Yes, that sin that you were on the very edge of committing! that angry word, and the angry feeling that makes you want to say it; that untrue word, and the cowardliness which makes you afraid to speak the exact truth; that proud look, and the naughty pride of heart that made it come into your eyes: Jesus stands by and says patiently and lovingly, "Put *that* on mine account!"

Can you bear that? does it not make you wish, ten times more than ever, to be kept from sinning against such a Saviour?

"Jesus, tender Saviour,
    Hast Thou died for me?
Make me very thankful
    In my heart to Thee;
When the sad, sad story
    Of Thy grief I read,
Make me very sorry
    For my sins indeed."

9.

WHITE GARMENTS.

"Let thy garments be always white."—Ecclesiastes 9:8.

"ALWAYS?" Oh, how can that be? They are soiled again directly after they
have been washed clean! Yet God says, "Let them be *always* white";
and He would not tell you to do what was impossible. Then how are you to help
soiling them? Only in one way. Last night's "little pillow" told you how Jesus
washes us "whiter than snow" in His own precious blood, that cleanseth from
all sin. But will He only cleanse His little one just for the moment? is that all
He is able and willing to do for you?

No; if you will only keep on trusting to that precious blood, and not turn
away from it, He says that it cleanseth, that is, *goes on cleansing.* You could not
keep your garments white for five minutes; careless thoughts would come like
dust upon them, and wrong words would make great dark stains, and before
long some naughty deed would be like a sad fall in the mud, and you would
feel sad and ashamed before the kind Saviour who still stands ready to cleanse
you again. But why should all this happen over and over again, till anybody but
our own loving, long-suffering Saviour would be tired of us, and give up doing any more for us? Why should it be, when His precious blood is meant to
"*go on cleansing*," so that our garments may be always white? Perhaps you never
thought of this; ask Him now this morning not only to wash you in the fountain of His precious blood, but *to keep you in it,* to *go on cleansing* you all day
long. *Trust* Him to do this, and see if it is not the happiest day you ever spent!

"And He can do all this for me,
Because in sorrow, on the tree,
He once for sinners hung;
And, having washed their sin away,
He now rejoices day by day,
To cleanse His little one."

10.

MADE BEAUTIFUL.

"Let the beauty of the Lord our God be upon us."—Psalm 90:17.

"HOW great is His beauty!" said Zechariah. How can His beauty be upon us? In two ways; try to understand them, and then ask that in both ways the beauty of the Lord our God may be upon you.

One way is by His covering you with the robe of Jesus Christ's righteousness, looking upon you not as you are in yourself, all sinful and unholy, but as if all the Saviour's beautiful and holy life were yours, reckoning it to you for His sake. In this way He can call us "perfect through my comeliness which I had put upon thee." The other way is by giving you the beauty of holiness, for that is His own beauty; and though we never can be quite like Him till we see Him as He is, He can begin to make us like Him even now. Look at a poor little colourless drop of water, hanging weakly on a blade of grass. It is not beautiful at all; why should you stop to look at it? Stay till the sun has risen, and now look. It is sparkling like a diamond; and if you look at it from another side, it will be glowing like a ruby, and presently gleaming like an emerald. The poor little drop has become one of the brightest and loveliest things you ever saw. But is it its own brightness and beauty? No; if it slipped down to the ground out of the sunshine, it would be only a poor little dirty drop of water. So, if the Sun of Righteousness, the glorious and lovely Saviour, shines upon you, a little ray of His own brightness and beauty will be seen upon you. Sometimes we can see by the happy light on a face that the Sun is shining there; but if the Sun is really shining, there are sure to be some of the beautiful rays of holiness, love, joy, peace, gentleness, goodness, faith, meekness, making the life even of a little child very lovely.

"Jesus, Lord, I come to Thee,
Thou hast said I may;
Tell me what my life should be,
Take my sins away.

"Jesus, Lord, I learn of Thee,
In Thy word divine;
Every promise there I see,
May I call it mine!"

11.

PLEASANT GIFTS.

"Who giveth us richly all things to enjoy."—1 Timothy 6:17.

THINK a little this morning of God's great kindness to you. How *very* good He is to you! I know one of His dear children who looks up many, many times a day, and says, "*Good* Lord Jesus!" or "*Kind* Lord Jesus!" She does not set herself to say it, but it seems as if she could not help saying it, just because He *is* so good and kind. And then it seems only natural to look up again and say, "*Dear* Lord Jesus!" How *can* anybody go on all day long, and never see how good He is, and never look up and bless Him? Most especially on bright pleasant days, when He giveth us more even than usual to enjoy! He "giveth." Not one single pleasant thing, not one single bit of enjoyment comes to us but what He giveth. We cannot get it, we do not earn it, we do not deserve it; but He *giveth* lovingly, and kindly, and freely. Suppose He stopped giving, what would become of us?

"Richly." So richly, that if you tried to write down half His gifts to you, your hand would be tired long before you had done. You might easily make a list of the presents given you on your birthday, but you could not make a list of what God gives you every day of your life.

"All things." All the things you really need, and a great many more besides. All the things that will do you good, a great many more than you would ever have thought of. All the things that He can fill your little hands with, and trust you to carry without stumbling and falling. *All* things, everything that you have at all!

"To enjoy." Now how kind this is! not only "to do us good," but "to enjoy." So you see He means you to be happy with what He gives you, to smile and laugh and be glad, not to be dismal and melancholy. If you do not enjoy what He "giveth," that is your own fault, for He meant you to enjoy it. Look up to Him with a bright smile and thank Him for having given you richly all things to enjoy!

> "My joys to Thee I bring,
> The joys Thy love hath given,
> That each may be a wing
> To lift me nearer heaven.
> I bring them, Saviour, all to Thee
> For Thou hast purchased all for me."

12.

MUCH MORE THAN THIS.

"The Lord is able to give thee much more than this."—2 Chronicles 25:9.

AMAZIAH, king of Judah, was going to war against the Edomites. He thought he would make sure of victory by hiring a hundred thousand soldiers from the King of Israel, and he paid them beforehand a hundred talents, which was about £34,218, 15s. of our money. But a man of God warned him not to let the army of Israel go with him, for Israel had forsaken the Lord, and so He was not with them. It seemed a great pity to waste all that money, and so Amaziah said, "But what shall we do for the hundred talents which I have given to the army of Israel? And the man of God answered, The Lord is able to give thee much more than this." So Amaziah simply obeyed, and sent the soldiers away, and trusted God to help him to do without them. Was it any wonder that he gained a great victory over the Edomites?

Does not this teach us that we should simply do the right thing, and trust God at any cost? When you do this, you will find that, in hundreds of ways which you never thought of, "the Lord is able to give thee much more." The trial comes in many different ways. One may be tempted to hurry over prayer and Bible, because there is something else that she very much wants to get done before breakfast, and she is afraid of not having time enough. Another shuts up her little purse when a call comes to give something for God's work, because she is afraid she will not have enough left for another purpose. Another is tempted to look at a key, or to glance over another's shoulder at a lesson, because without it he would not get the marks he is trying for. Another is tempted not to tell the exact truth, or to conceal something which he ought to tell, because he would lose something by it. Oh, resist the devil, and do what you know is right, and trust God for all the rest! For "the Lord is able to give thee much more than this," whatever your "*this*" may be. And His smile and His blessing will always be "more than this," more than anything else!

> "Be brave to do the right,
>   And scorn to be untrue;
> When fear would whisper 'yield!'
>   Ask, 'What would Jesus do?'"

13.

THE DOINGS OF THE KING.

"Whatsoever the king did pleased all the people."—2 Samuel 3:36.

DAVID had been giving a proof of his love for one who had long been his enemy, but whom he had received into friendship; and he had been giving a proof of his tender-heartedness and sympathy with the people, by weeping with them at the grave of Abner. "And all the people took notice of it, and it pleased them: as whatsoever the king did pleased all the people."

This was because they loved their king. They watched him, not as the wicked Pharisees watched the Lord Jesus that they might find something against Him; but with the watching of admiration and love, taking notice of the kind and gracious things he did and said. Do you thus take notice of what your King does? Does it please you to hear and read of what He has done and what He is doing? It must be so if He really is your King.

But the "whatsoever" is a little harder; and yet, if it is once really learnt, it makes everything easy. For if we learn to be pleased with *whatsoever* our King Jesus does, nothing can come wrong to us.

Suppose something comes to-day which is not quite what you would have liked; heavy rain, for instance, when you wanted to go out,—recollect that your King Jesus has done it, and that will hush the little murmur, and make you quite content. Ask Him this morning to make you so loving and loyal to Him, that *whatsoever* He does, all day long, may please you, because it has pleased Him to do it. I think He loves us so much, that He always gives us as much happiness as He can possibly trust us with, and does what is pleasantest for His dear children whenever He sees it will not hurt them; so, when He does something which at first does not seem so pleasant, we may still trust our beloved King, and learn by His grace to be pleased with *whatsoever* He does.

"I hear a sweet voice ringing clear,
'All is well!'
It is my Father's voice I hear,
All is well!
Where'er I walk that voice is heard,
It is my God, my Father's word—
'Fear not, but trust; I am the Lord,
All is well.'"

14.

THE NEW HEART.

"A new heart also will I give you."—Ezekiel 36:26.

WHY does God promise this? Because our old hearts are so evil that they cannot be made any better; and so nothing will do any good but giving us a quite new heart.

Because we cannot make a new heart for ourselves; the more we try, the more we shall find we cannot do it; so God, in His great pity and kindness, says He will give it us.

Because unless we have a new heart we cannot enter the kingdom of God, we cannot even see it! Without this gift we must be left outside in the terrible darkness when "the door is shut."

What is the difference? The old heart *likes* to be naughty in some way or other; either it likes to be idle, or it likes to let out sharp words, or to go on being sulky or fretful instead of clearing up and saying, "I am sorry!" The new heart wants to be good; and is grieved when a temptation comes, and does not wish to yield to it; and would like to be always pleasing the Saviour.

The old heart is afraid of God, and does not love Him, and would much rather He were not always seeing us. And it does not care to hear about Jesus, but would rather be just let alone. The new heart loves God and trusts what He says, and likes to know that He is always watching it. And it is glad to hear about Jesus, and wants to come closer to Him.

The old heart is a little slave of Satan, taking his orders, and doing what he wishes. The new heart is a happy little servant of Christ, listening to His orders, and doing what He wishes.

Oh how happy and blessed to have this new heart! All God's own children receive it, for He has said, "I will give them one heart"; that is, all the same new heart. Do you not want to have it too? Then "ask, and you *shall* receive"; for He hath said, "A new heart also *will* I give you!"

> "Oh for a heart to praise my God,
>   A heart from sin set free!
> A heart that always feels Thy blood,
>   So freely shed for me.
>
> "A heart resigned, submissive, meek,
>   My dear Redeemer's throne;
> Where only Christ is heard to speak,
>   Where Jesus reigns alone."

15.

THE GIFT OF THE HOLY SPIRIT.

"I will put my Spirit within you."—Ezekiel 36:27.

MANY years ago a good clergyman wrote a tiny prayer, so short that no one could help remembering it if they once heard it. God seemed to set that little prayer "upon wheels," so that it might run everywhere. It was printed on large cards and hung up, and it was printed on small ones and kept in Bibles and pocket-books. It was taught to classes, and schools, and whole congregations, and now thousands upon thousands pray it constantly. It is a prayer which must be heard, because it asks for what God has promised to give; and it asks for this through Him whom the Father heareth always. It is this. "O God, give me Thy Holy Spirit, for Jesus Christ's sake. Amen." Will you not pray it too? Begin this morning, and go on, not just *saying* it, but *praying* it, till you get a full answer. For you are quite sure to get it; here is God's own promise, "I *will* put my Spirit within you"; and He has promised it over and over again in other places. Perhaps you will not know at first when the answer comes. Can you see the dew fall? No one ever saw a single drop come down, and yet as soon as the sun rises, you see that it has come, and is sparkling all over the fields. It came long before you saw it, falling sweetly and silently in the twilight and in the dark. So do not fancy God is not hearing you because you have not felt anything very sudden and wonderful. He is hearing and answering all the time. You would not go on asking unless the dew of His Spirit were already falling upon your heart, and teaching you to pray. The more He gives you of His blessed Spirit, the more you will ask for; and the more you ask, the more He will give.

> "Thou gift of Jesus, now descend,
>   And be my Comforter and Friend;
>   O Holy Spirit, fill my heart,
>   That I from Christ may ne'er depart!
>
> "Show me my soul all black within,
>   And cleanse and keep me pure within;
>   Oh, show me Jesus! let me rest
>   My heart upon His loving breast!"

16.

HOW TO CONQUER.

"The Lord shall fight for you."—Exodus 14:14.

HOW glad the children of Israel must have been when Moses said these words to them on the shores of the Red Sea! For when they "lifted up their eyes, behold, the Egyptians marched after them; and they were sore afraid."

The Egyptians had been cruel masters to them; and they had horses and chariots to pursue them with; and there was the sea close before them, and no boats! Perhaps some of the Israelites thought it was no use trying to escape, they only would be overtaken and conquered, and be worse off than before. And so, left to themselves, they would have been; but God fought for them in a way they never thought of. For "the Lord saved Israel that day out of the hand of the Egyptians, and Israel saw the Egyptians dead upon the seashore."

What about your Egyptians?—the angry tempers or sulky looks, the impatient words, the vain and foolish thoughts, the besetting sins that master you so often. Have you tried so often to fight against them, and failed, that it seems almost no use, and you do not see how to conquer them or to escape them? Are you very tired of fighting, and "sore afraid" of being always overcome just the same as ever? Now hear God's true, strong promise to you. "The Lord shall fight for you!" "Will He really?" Yes, really, and He will conquer for you too, if you will only believe His Word and trust the battle to Him, and *let* Him fight for you.

How? First, watch! and then the very instant you see the enemy coming, look up and say, "Come, Lord and fight for me"; and keep on looking up and *expecting* Him to fight for you. And *you will find* that He does fight for you and gives you the victory; and you too will be "saved that day," and will see "the Egyptians dead upon the sea-shore." Try Him, and trust Him; and you, even you, will be "more than conqueror through Him that loved you."

> "So, when you meet with trials,
>   And know not what to do;
> Just cast the care on Jesus,
>   And He will fight for you.
> Gird on the heavenly armour
>   Of faith, and hope, and love;
> And when the conflict's ended,
>   You'll reign with Him above."

17.

THE MASTER'S VOICE.

"I will watch to see what He will say unto me."—Habakkuk 2:1.

WHEN the Lord Jesus said to Simon the Pharisee, "Simon, I have some-what to say unto thee"; he answered, "Master say on!" When God was going to speak to Samuel, he said, "Speak, Lord, for Thy servant heareth." Has the Lord Jesus said anything like this for us? He says, "I have yet many things to say unto you." What things? They will be strong, helpful, life-giving words, for He says, "The words that I speak unto you, they are spirit and they are life." They will be very loving words, for He says, "I will speak comfortably to her" (margin, "I will speak to her heart"). And they will be very kind and tender words, and spoken just at the right moment, for He says that He knows "how to speak a word in season to him that is weary." "Will He really speak to me?" says the little heart. Yes, really, if you will only watch to see what He will say to you. For it will be "a still, small voice," and you will not hear it at all if you do not listen for it. "How will He speak to me?" If I had something very nice to tell you, and instead of saying it out loud, I wrote it down on a piece of paper and gave it you to look at, would not that be exactly the same as if I had told it you with my lips? And you would take the paper eagerly to see what it was that I had to say to you. So to-day, when you read your Bible, either alone or at your Bible lesson, watch to see what Jesus will say to you in it. You will never really watch in vain. You will see some word that seems to come home to you, and that you never noticed so much before. Oh, listen lovingly to it, for *that* is what He says to you! Or if you are really watching and wishing for a word from Him, some sweet text will come into your mind, and you wonder what made you think of it! That is the voice of Jesus speaking to your heart. Listen to it, and treasure it up, and follow it; and then watch to see what else He will say to you. Say to Him "Master, say on!"

"Master, speak! and make me ready,
When Thy voice is truly heard,
With obedience glad and steady
Still to follow every word.
I am listening, Lord, for Thee;
Master, speak, oh speak to me!"

18.

WHO WILL TAKE CARE OF ME?

"He careth for you."—1 Peter 5:7.

IT is so pleasant to be cared for; to have kind relations and friends who show that they love you by their care of you, and their care for you. What would you do if no one cared for you, like the poor little children in London who are turned out to "do for themselves" before they are as old as you are? What would you do if there was no one to get anything for you to eat, or to see to your clothes, or to keep a home for you to live in? No one to take any notice if you hurt yourself ever so badly, or if you were ever so ill? You would feel then what a difference being cared for makes to your life. But all the earthly care for you comes because "He careth for you." He planned and arranged everything, without your having anything to do with it, so that you shall be cared for. And He did not arrange it once for all, and then leave things to go on as might happen. No! Every day, every moment, He careth, *goes on* caring, for you. Not only thinking of you and watching you, but working for you; making things come right, so that everything should be just the best that could happen to you. Not managing the great things, and leaving the little things to arrange themselves; but giving loving care to the least, the very least things that concern you. Even in some tiny little trouble which no one else seems to care about, "He careth"; or when every one else is too much taken up with other things to attend to you, "He careth for you."

You can never get beyond God's care, for it always reaches you; you can never be outside of it, for it is always enfolding you.

> "'Who will take care of me?' darling, you say,
>   Lovingly, tenderly watched as you are!
> Listen! I give you the answer to-day,
>   ONE who is never forgetful or far.
>
> "He will take care of you! All through the year
>   Crowning each day with His kindness and love,
> Sending you blessings and shielding from fear,
>   Leading you on to His bright home above."

19.

UNDER HIS WINGS.

"Under His wings shalt thou trust."—Psalm 91:4.

THAT means to-day, not some other time! Under His wings, the shadowing wings of the Most High, you, poor little helpless one, are to trust to-day.

When the little eaglets, that have not yet a feather to fly with, are under the great wings of the parent eagle, how safe they are! Who would dare touch them? If a bold climber put his hand into the nest then, those powerful wings would beat him in a minute from his hold, and he would fall down the rocks and be dashed to pieces. So safe shall you be "under His wings," "nothing shall by any means hurt you" there.

When the wild snow-storms rage round the eyrie, and the mountain cold is felt, that is death to an unprotected sleeper, how warm the little eaglets are kept! Not an arrow of the keen blast reaches them, poor little featherless things, not a snowflake touches them. So warm shall you be kept "under His wings," when any cold and dark day of trouble comes, or even any sudden little blast of unkindness or loneliness.

"Under His wings shalt thou *trust!*" Not "shalt thou *see!*" If one of the eaglets wanted to see for itself what was going on, and thought it could take care of itself for a little while, and hopped from under the shadow of the wings, it would be neither safe nor warm. The sharp wind would chill it, and the cruel hand might seize it then. So you are to *trust,* rest quietly and peacefully, "under His wings"; stay there, not be peeping out and wondering whether God really is taking care of you! You may be always safe and happy there. Safe, for "in the shadow of Thy wings will I make my refuge." Happy, for "in the shadow of Thy wings will I rejoice."

Remember, too, that it is a command as well as a promise; it is what you are to do to-day, all day long: "Under His wings *shalt* thou trust!"

> "I am trusting Thee, Lord Jesus,
>   Trusting only Thee!
> Trusting Thee for full salvation,
>   Great and free.
>
> "I am trusting Thee to guide me,
>   Thou alone shalt lead!
> Every day and hour supplying
>   All my need."

20.

ALWAYS NEAR.

"I am with you alway."—Matthew 28:20.

HOW nice it would be if we could always have the one we loved best in all the world with us; never away from us night or day, and no fear that they ever possibly would or could leave us; never a good-bye even for ever such a little while, and never, never the long farewell of death!

Can this ever be for you? Yes, for you; for to every one who is a disciple of the Lord Jesus (that is, who learns of Him and owns Him as Master), He says, "I am with you alway." He does not even say, "I will be with you"; so that you might be wondering when He meant to come, when He would begin to be "with you"; but He says, "I *am* with you." Yes, even now, though perhaps your eyes are holden, like those of the two who walked to Emmaus, when Jesus was beside them and they did not know it. Your feeling or not feeling that He is there has nothing at all to do with it, because His word must be true and *is* true, and He has said, "I *am* with you alway." All you have to do is to be happy in believing it to be true. And if you go on believing it, you will soon begin to realize it; that is, to find that it is a real thing, and that Jesus really is with you.

How long will He be with you? Always, "all the days!" He hath said, "I will never leave thee." "Never" means really never, not for one moment. You cannot get beyond "never." It goes on all through your life, and all through God's great "forever." And "always" means really *always*, every single moment of all your life, so that you need never ask again, "Is Jesus with me now?" Of course He is! the answer will always be "yes," because He hath said, "I am with you alway." How safe, how sweet, how blessed!

> "O Jesus, make Thyself to me
> A living, bright reality!
> More present to faith's vision keen
> Than any outward object seen;
> More dear, more intimately nigh,
> Than even the sweetest earthly tie."

21.

DOING GOD'S WILL

"Teach me to do Thy will."—Psalm 143:10.

WHEN you see some one doing with very great delight some beautiful and pleasant piece of work, have you not thought, "I should like to be able to do that!" and perhaps you have said, "Please, teach me how to do it."

Can you think of anything pleasanter to do than what the very angels are full of delight in doing? Can you think of anything more beautiful to do than what is done in the "pleasant land," the beautiful home above? Can you fancy anything more interesting to do than what the dwellers there will never get tired of doing for thousands of millions of years? Would you not like to be taught to do it too?—to begin the pleasant and beautiful and most interesting work now, instead of waiting till you are grown up, and then perhaps never learning it at all, because it was put off now? Then pray this little prayer this morning with all your heart, "Teach me to do Thy will." For it is His will that is the happiest work above, and the very happiest thing to do here below.

What is His will? The Prayer-Book version of this Psalm tells you very simply and sweetly. It says, "Teach me to do the thing that pleaseth Thee." So doing God's will is just doing the things, one by one, that please Him.

Why did David ask this? He goes on to say why—"For Thou art my God." If God is really our God we too shall wish to do the thing that pleaseth Him. David did not think he could do it of himself, for he says next, "Let Thy loving Spirit lead me." That loving Spirit will lead you too, dear child, and show you how beautiful and grand God's will is, and make you long to do it always, and teach you to do it. So that even on earth you may begin to do what the angels are doing in heaven!

> "It is but very little
> For Him that I can do,
> Then let me seek to serve Him,
> My earthly journey through;
> And without sigh or murmur,
> To do His holy will;
> And in my daily duties
> His wise commands fulfil."

22.

WORKING FOR JESUS.

"Ye have done it unto me." "Ye did it not to me."—Matthew 25:40, 45.

OUR Lord Jesus Christ has given us opportunities of showing whether we love Him or not. He tells us that what we try to do for anyone who is poor, or hungry, or sick, or a lonely stranger, is just the same as doing it to Him. And when the King says, "Come, ye blessed," He will remember these little things, and will say, "Ye have done it unto Me." But He tells us that if we do nothing for them, it is just the same as if He were standing there and we would do nothing for Him. And He will say, "Ye did it not to me."

One of these two words will be spoken to you in the great day when you see the King on the throne of His glory. Which shall it be? What are you doing for Jesus? Are you doing anything at all for Him? Perhaps you say, "I have no opportunity." Did you ever try to find one? Did you ever ask Him to give you opportunities of doing something for Him? Or is it only that you have never yet cared or tried to do anything for Him? Be honest about it. He knows. And He will forgive.

But now, what is to be done? Begin by asking Him to show you. And then, keep a bright, sharp lookout, and see if you cannot find an opportunity very soon (and perhaps many) of doing something kind for His sake to some poor or sick or lonely one. Set to work to *think* what you could do!

It seems to me so very kind of the Lord Jesus to have told us this. For He knew that those who really love Him would *want* to do something for Him, and what could we do for the King of glory in His glorious heaven? So it was wonderfully thoughtful of Him to give us His poor people to care for, and to say, if we have only been kind to a sick old woman or hungry little child, "Ye have done it unto me!"

> "I love my precious Saviour
>   Because He died for me;
> And if I did not serve Him,
>   How sinful I should be!
> God help me to be useful
>   In all I do or say!
> I mean to work for Jesus,
>   The Bible says I may!"

23.

STANDARD-BEARERS.

"Thou hast given a banner to them that fear Thee."—Psalm 60:4.

THEN what is your banner, and what are you doing with it? For if you are among "them that fear" God, He has given you a banner "that it may be displayed." Is yours furled up and put away in a corner, so that nobody sees it or knows of it? Or are you trying to be a brave little standard bearer of Jesus Christ, carrying His flag, so that the sweet breezes of His Spirit may lift its bright folds, and show its golden motto? That motto, I think, is "Love." For we are told that His banner over us is love. Are you displaying it, showing your love to Him by your love to others? showing the power of His love over you by your sweet, happy temper, and by trying to please Him always?

Carrying a banner means something. First, it means that you belong to or have to do with those whose banner you carry, and that you are not ashamed of them. At great Sunday-school festivals we know to which school a boy belongs by the flag that he carries. You would like to carry the flag of England or the Queen's royal flag, because you are English and loyal. So let us carry the banner of Jesus Christ because we are loyal to Him, and are not ashamed to own Him as our King. Secondly, it means that we are ready to fight, and ready to encourage others to fight under the same banner. When you are tempted to do something wrong, remember whose banner you carry, and do not disgrace it. If one does right, it makes it easier for the other to do right too. Thirdly, it means rejoicing. You know how flags are hung out on grand days, and carried in triumphal processions. The little hand that carries Christ's banner through His war, will carry it also in His triumph; the little hand that tries to unfurl it bravely now, will wave it when His glorious reign begins and His blessed kingdom is come. Then, "in the name of our God we will set up our banners" *now!*

"The Master hath called us, the children who fear Him,
Who march 'neath Christ's banner, His own little band;
We love Him, and seek Him; we long to be near Him,
And rest in the light of His beautiful land."

24.

SOLDIERS.

"Chosen to be a soldier."—2 Timothy 2:4.

ARE you a soldier? You ought to be, for you have been chosen to be a soldier in the glorious army of Jesus Christ.

You ought to be, for you have been "received into the congregation of Christ's flock" at your baptism, and engaged "manfully to fight under His banner against sin, the world, and the devil, and to continue Christ's faithful soldier and servant unto your life's end." You can never undo that, even if you are a deserter, and found in the enemy's ranks. The Captain of our salvation will not undo it, for He is ready to receive you, if you will but come and enlist now. Now, this very morning, come and enlist! This very morning ask Him to receive you into His noble army, and to give you first the shield of His salvation, and then the whole armour of God, and to "teach your hands to war and your fingers to fight," and to give you victories every day even now, and to let you share His grand triumphs hereafter.

Perhaps you know that you have enlisted already, you know and love your Captain, and He is enabling you, even if very feebly, yet really, to fight the good fight of faith? How came you to enlist? Was it any credit to you? Oh no! it was all His doing. It was He who chose you to be a soldier, not you who chose Him to be a Captain. And then He sent not some dreadful cannon-roar, but the sweet bugle-call of His love, to win you to join His ranks. And now He fights not only with you, but for you. In His war "nothing shall by any means hurt you," for "He was wounded" for you. Your life is safe with Him, for He laid down His own for you. By His side you can never be vanquished, because He goes forth "always conquering and to conquer."

> "Stand up, stand up for Jesus!
> Ye soldiers of the cross;
> Lift high His royal banner,
> It must not suffer loss.

> "From victory to victory
> His army shall be led,
> Till every foe is vanquished,
> And Christ is Lord indeed.

> "Stand up, stand up for Jesus!
> The trumpet call obey;
> Forth to the mighty conflict,
> In this His glorious day!"

25.

A LOYAL AIM.

"That he may please him who hath chosen him to be a soldier."—2 Timothy 2:4.

HERE is something worth aiming at, worth trying for! The Lord Jesus, the Captain of our salvation, is He who hath chosen us to be His soldiers; and now, does He only tell us that we may do our duty,—serve, obey, and fight? No; He tells us something more, gives us a hope and an aim so bright and pleasant, that it is like sunshine upon everything. He says, we "may *please* Him."

Only one who knows what it is to mourn for having grieved the dear Saviour, can quite understand what a happy word this is! That we, who have been cold, and careless, and sinful, grieving His love over and over again, should be told after all that we may *please* Him! Oh, if we love Him, our hearts will just leap at the hope of it! Perhaps we thought this could not be till we reached heaven; but you see His own word says, we "may please Him" now, while we are soldiers, in the very midst of the fighting. St. Paul tells us one thing in which you may please Him: "Children, obey your parents in all things, for this is well-pleasing unto the Lord." But he prays too that the Colossians "might walk worthy of the Lord unto *all* pleasing."

Shall this be your aim and your hope to-day? Will you look up to the Lord Jesus now, and ask Him first to give you the faith without which "it is impossible to please Him," and then to show you "how you ought to walk and to please God," and so to help you to "do those things that are pleasing in His sight"; that all your ways, even every little step of your ways, may really and truly "please the Lord" (Proverbs 16:7).

> "True-hearted, whole-hearted, faithful, and loyal,
>   King of our lives, by Thy grace we will be;
> Under Thy standard, exalted and royal,
>   Strong in Thy strength, we will battle for Thee.

> "True-hearted, whole-hearted! Fullest allegiance,
>   Yielding henceforth to our glorious King,
> Valiant endeavour and loving obedience,
>   Freely and joyously now we would bring."

26.

OBEDIENCE TO CHRIST.

"Whatsoever He saith unto you, do it."—John 2:5.

HOW are you to know what He says to you? Ah, it is so easy to know if we are really willing to know, and willing to obey when we do know! He has spoken so plainly to us in His word! In that He tells us, tells even little children, exactly what to do. It is most wonderful how He has said everything there for us, told us everything we ought to do. When you read a chapter or hear one read, listen and watch to see what He saith unto you in it. There is another way in which He tells us what to do. Do you not hear a little voice inside that always tells you to do the right thing and not to do the wrong thing? That is conscience, and He speaks to you by it.

Another way is by those whom He has set over you. He has told you once for all to "obey your parents," and to "obey them that have the rule over you." So, when they tell you to do something, it is the Lord Jesus Himself that you have to obey in obeying them.

Now "whatsoever He saith unto you, do it!" Yes, "whatsoever," dear little one, whether easy or hard, do it because He tells you; do it for love of Him, and it will be a thousand times better and happier to obey your King than to please yourself. And He Himself will help you to do it; only look up to Him for grace to obey, and He will give it.

"Whatsoever He saith unto you, *do* it." Do not just think about doing it, or talk about doing it, but *do* it! "Do *it!*" Do the exact thing He would have you do, not something a little bit different, or something which you think will be very nearly the same, but do "*it.*"

And "do it" at once. It is so true, that "the very first moment is the easiest for obedience." Every minute that you put off doing the right thing makes it harder. Do not let your King have to "speak twice" to you. "Whatsoever He saith unto you, do it cheerfully, exactly, and instantly."

> "Jesus, help me, I am weak;
>   Let me put my trust in Thee;
> Teach me how and what to speak;
>   Loving Saviour, care for me.
> Dear Saviour, hear me,
>   Hear a little child to-day;
> Hear, oh hear me;
>   Hear me when I pray."

27.

DO IT HEARTILY.

"Whatsoever ye do, do it heartily, as to the Lord."—Colossians 3:23.

IN 2 Chronicles 31:21, we read of Hezekiah, that "in every work that he began, he did it with all his heart, and prospered." And this morning's "bell" rings a New Testament echo, "Do it heartily!" Sing it now, like a little peal of bells!

Do   it   hear- ti- ly!

See if that does not ring in your ears all day, and remind you that it is not merely much pleasanter to be bright and brisk about everything, but that it is actually one of God's commands, written in His own word.

I know this is easier to some than to others. Perhaps it "comes natural" to you to do everything heartily. That is very nice, but it is not enough. What else? "Whatsoever ye do, do it heartily, *as unto the Lord*, and not unto men." He knows whether the industrious, energetic boy or girl is wishing to please Him, and looking up to Him for His smile; or whether He is forgotten all the while, and only the smile of others and the pleasure of being quick and busy is thought of. But perhaps it is hard for you to do things heartily. You like better to take your time, and so you dawdle, and do things in an idle way, especially what you do not much like doing. Is this right? Is it a little sin, when God's word says, "Whatsoever ye do, do it heartily"? Is it not just as much disobeying God as breaking any other command? Are you not *guilty* before Him? Very likely you never thought of it in this way, but there the words stand, and neither you nor I can alter them. First ask Him to forgive you all the past idleness and idle ways, for Christ's sake, and then ask Him to give you strength henceforth to obey this word of His. And then listen to the little chime, "Do it heartily! do it heartily!" And then the last word of the verse about Hezekiah will be true of you too—"Prospered!"

"Up and doing, little Christian!
   Up and doing, while 'tis day!
  Do the work the Master gives you,
   Do not loiter by the way.

For we all have work before us,
   You, dear child, as well as I;
  Let us learn to seek our duty,
   And to 'do it heartily.'"

28.

THE SIGHT OF FAITH.

"As seeing Him who is invisible."—Hebrews 11:27.

I F we were always doing everything just as if we saw Him, whom having not seen we love, how different our lives would be! How much happier too! How brave, and bright, and patient we should be, if all the time we could really see Jesus as Stephen saw Him! And by faith, the precious faith which God is ready to give to all who ask, we may go on our way with this light upon it, "as seeing Him who is invisible."

These words were said of Moses; and this seeing Him by faith had three effects. First, "he forsook Egypt"; it made him ready to give up anything for his God, and God's people. It made him true and loyal to God's cause. What did he care for anything else, so long as he saw "Him who is invisible"? Secondly, it took away all his fear. What was "the wrath of the king" to him, when Jehovah was by his side? Of what should he be afraid? Thirdly, it enabled him to "endure," to wait patiently for forty years in the desert, and then to work patiently for forty years in the wilderness; and only think how strength-giving that sight of faith must be which enabled him to endure everything for eighty years!

Try for yourself to-day what was such great and long help to Moses. Ask God, before you go down-stairs, for faith, "the eye of the soul," so that you may walk all day long "as seeing Him who is invisible." When you are tempted to indulge in something wrong,—idleness or carelessness, or selfishness,—this will help you to give it up at once, and forsake it; for how can you give way to it when your eye meets His? When something makes you afraid, this will make you brave and peaceful; for how can you fear anything when your God is so near? When lessons, or work, or even having to be quiet with nothing to do, seem very tiresome, and you are tempted to be impatient, and perhaps cross, this will help you to endure, and not only so, but to feel patient; for how can you be impatient when you are looking up to Him, and He is looking down on you all the time!

"God will not leave me all alone,
He never will forsake His own;
When not another friend I see,
The Lord is looking down on me."

29.

NO WEIGHTS.

"Let us lay aside every weight."—Hebrews 12:1.

IF you were going to run a race, you would first put down all the parcels you might have been carrying. And if you had a heavy little parcel in your pocket, you would take that out, and lay it down too, because it would hinder you in running. You would know better than to say, "I will put down the parcels which I have in my hands, but nobody can see the one in my pocket, so that one won't matter!" You would "lay aside *every* weight."

You have a race to run to-day, a little piece of the great race that is set before you. God has set a splendid prize before you, "the prize of the high calling of God in Christ Jesus," a crown that is incorruptible.

Now what are you going to do about the weights, the things that hinder you from running this race? You know some things do seem to hinder you; will you keep them or lay them aside? Will you only lay aside something that every one can see is hindering you, so that you will get a little credit for putting it down, and keep something that your own little conscience knows is a real hindrance, though no one else knows anything at all about it? Oh, take St. Paul's wise and holy advice, and make up your mind to lay aside *every* weight.

Different persons have different weights; we must find out what ours are, and give them up. One finds that if she does not get up directly she is called, the time slips by, and there is not enough left for quiet prayer and Bible reading. Then here is a little weight that must be laid aside. Another is at school, and finds that he gets no good, but a little harm, when he goes much with a certain boy. Then he must lay that weight aside. Another takes a story-book up to bed, and reads it while nurse is brushing her hair, and up to the last minute, and then her head is so full of the story that she only *says words* when she kneels down, and cannot really *pray* at all. Can she doubt that this is a weight which must be laid aside?

It may seem hard to lay our pet weight down; but oh, if you only knew how light we feel when it is laid down, and how much easier it is to run the race which God has set before us!

30.

THE SHIELD OF SALVATION.

"Thou hast also given me the shield of Thy salvation."—2 Samuel 22:36.

THIS beautiful little text teaches us a very precious truth. It shows us that the salvation which the Lord Jesus came to bring is not only salvation at last, just escaping hell, but that it is salvation now, and salvation in everything. Salvation does not only mean victory at last, but it is like a broad shining shield, given to us in the midst of the battle, coming between us and the poisoned arrows and sharp sword-thrusts of the enemy. It is a shield not only to keep us from death, but to keep us from being hurt and wounded. It is the shield which the Captain *has* given us to use now, as well as the crown which He *will* give when the warfare is ended.

How are you to use this shield? what does it really mean for you? It means, that if you have come to the Lord Jesus to be saved, He does not merely say He *will* save you, but that you *are* saved, that He saves you now. And this is how you are to use it—believe it, and be sure of it, because you have His word for it; and then, when a temptation comes, tell the enemy that he has nothing to do with you, for you are saved; that you belong to Jesus, and not to him,—look up and say, "Jesus saves me!" Will He fail you? Did He ever let any find themselves deceived and mistaken who looked up in faith and confidence to Him, trusting in His great salvation? Never! and never will you find this shield of His salvation fail to cover you completely. Satan himself cannot touch you when you are behind this shield! Lift it up when you see him coming, even ever so far off, and you will be safe.

> "Jesus saves me every day,
>   Jesus saves me every night;
> Jesus saves me all the way,
>   Through the darkness, through the light."

31.

I WILL LOVE THEE.

"I will love Thee, O Lord."—Psalm 18:1.

YES, even if I have never loved Thee before, I will love Thee, O Lord, now! I will love Thee, Lord Jesus, because Thou hast loved me, and because Thou art loving me now, and wilt love me to the end. Oh forgive me for not having loved Thee! How could I have helped loving Thee, when Thou wast waiting all the time for me, waiting so patiently while I did not care about Thee! Oh forgive me! and now I will love Thee always; for Thou wilt take my love, and fix it on Thyself, and keep it for Thyself.

I will love Thee, O Lord Jesus; I will not listen to Satan, who tries to keep me from loving Thee; I will not ask myself anything about it, lest I should begin to get puzzled about whether I do love Thee or not. Thou knowest that I do want to love Thee, and now, dear Lord Jesus, hear me say that I *will* love Thee, and that I will trust Thee to make me love Thee more and more, always more and more.

I have said it, dear Lord Jesus, and Thou hast heard me say it. And I am so glad I have said it, I do not want ever to take it back, and Thou wilt not let me take it back. I am to love Thee always now; and Thou wilt give me Thy Holy Spirit to shed abroad Thy love in my heart, so that it may be filled with love. Fill me so full of Thy love that it may run over into everything I do, and that I may love everybody, because I love Thee.

Yes, I will love Thee, dear Lord Jesus!

"My Saviour, I love Thee, I know Thou art mine!
For Thee all the follies of sin I resign;
My gracious Redeemer, my Saviour art Thou;
If ever I loved Thee, my Saviour, 'tis now!

I love Thee, because Thou hast first lovèd me,
And purchased my pardon on Calvary's tree;
I love Thee for wearing the thorns on Thy brow;
If ever I loved Thee, my Saviour, 'tis now!

I will love Thee in life, I will love Thee in death,
And praise Thee as long as Thou lendest me breath;
And say, when the death-dew lies cold on my brow,
If ever I loved Thee, my Saviour, 'tis now."

Chapters learnt by F. R. H.

Genesis. 1. Learnt in Hebrew
       Sept. 1856.
Isaiah. 1. ditto. Aug. 1856
— 4 Learnt. March. 1852.
— 12. Learnt. 1846.
— 35 Learnt 1847.
— 40 Learnt 1849
— 53. Learnt 1846.
— 55. Learnt 1846.
— 63. Learnt 1852.

The Epistle to the Romans
Finished learning Dec. 1854
Relearnt. Nov. 1857,
Galatians, finished learning
      Feby 6th 1858

Epistle to the Hebrews
    Finished learning Oct 24, 1857
Epistle of James
    Finished learning. Nov. 9. 1857.
1st Epistle of Peter
    Finished learning, Nov. 25. 1857.
2nd Epistle of Peter
    Finished learning Dec. 5, 1857
1st Epistle of St. John
    Finished learning Dec 22 1857.
2nd Epistle of St. John
    Learnt Dec. 24. 1857.
3rd Epistle of John
    Learnt Dec 26 1857

Epistle of Jude
    Learnt Dec. 30. 1857.
Revelation, chapters 1 — 6
    Learnt July 1852

Many other chapters are
scored with dates, but as it
is not stated that they were
learnt they have not been
added to this list.

This list was found among Havergal manuscripts and papers, likely gathered and written by one of her three sisters. We also know from her sister Maria that F.R.H. memorized all the New Testament except the Book of Acts, all the Minor Prophets, Isaiah, and all the Psalms.

them that call on the Lord out of a pure heart.

23 But foolish and unlearned questions avoid, knowing that they do gender strifes.

24 And the servant of the Lord must not strive; but be gentle unto all *men*, apt to teach, patient,

25 In meekness instructing those that oppose themselves; if God peradventure will give them repentance to the acknowledging of the truth;

26 And *that* they may recover themselves out of the snare of the devil, who are taken captive by him at his will.

CHAPTER III.

THIS know also, that in the last days perilous times shall come.

2 For men shall be lovers of their own selves, covetous, boasters, proud, blasphemers, disobedient to parents, unthankful, unholy,

3 Without natural affection, trucebreakers, false accusers, incontinent, fierce, despisers of those that are good,

4 Traitors, heady, highminded, lovers of pleasures more than lovers of God;

5 Having a form of godliness, but denying the power thereof: from such turn away.

6 For of this sort are they which creep into houses, and lead captive silly women laden with sins, led away with divers lusts,

7 Ever learning, and never able to come to the knowledge of the truth.

8 Now as Jannes and Jambres withstood Moses, so do these also resist the truth: men of corrupt minds, reprobate concerning the faith.

9 But they shall proceed no further: for their folly shall be manifest unto all *men*, as their's also was.

10 But thou hast fully known my doctrine, manner of life, purpose, faith, longsuffering, charity, patience,

11 Persecutions, afflictions, which came unto me at Antioch, at Iconium, at Lystra; what persecutions I endured: but out of *them* all the Lord delivered me.

12 Yea, and all that will live godly in Christ Jesus shall suffer persecution.

13 But evil men and seducers shall wax worse and worse, deceiving, and being deceived.

14 But continue thou in the things which thou hast learned and hast been assured of, knowing of whom thou hast learned *them*;

15 And that from a child thou hast known the holy scriptures, which are able to make thee wise unto salvation through faith which is in Christ Jesus.

16 All scripture *is* given by inspiration of God, and *is* profitable for doctrine, for reproof, for correction, for instruction in righteousness;

17 That the man of God may be perfect, throughly furnished unto all good works.

CHAPTER IV.

I CHARGE thee therefore before God, and the Lord Jesus Christ, who shall

155

A. D. 66.

a 1 Co. 1. 2.
b Re. 20. 12, 13
c verse 16.
d Tit. 2. 15.
β or, *forbearing*.
e Ga. 6. 1.
f Ac. 8. 22.
g Tit. 1. 1.
γ *awake*.
h 1 Ti. 1. 4.
i 1 Ti. 3. 7.
k chap. 2. 3.
δ *alive*.
ζ or, *fulfil*.
l 1 Ti. 4. 12, 15.
m 1 Ti. 4. 1.
2 Pe. 3. 3.
1 John 2. 18.
Jude 17, 18.
n Phi. 1. 23.
2 Pe. 1. 14.
o Ro. 1. 29. .31.
p 1 Ti. 6. 12.
q Ac. 20. 24.
η or, *makebate*.
r Pr. 23. 23.
Re. 3. 10.
s 1 Co. 9. 25.
1 Pe. 5. 4.
Re. 2. 10.
t 2 Pe. 2. 10,
&c.
u Phi. 3. 19.
v 1 Co. 2. 9.
w Tit. 1. 16.
x 1 John 2. 15.
y Tit. 1. 11.
z Tit. 3. 12.
a Ex. 7. 11.
b 1 Ti. 6. 5.
θ or, *of no judgment*.
c Ps. 23. 4.
κ or, *been a diligent follower of*.
λ or, *preachings*.
d Ac. 13. 45, 50
e Ac. 14. 5, 6,
19.
f chap. 1. 15.
g Ac. 7. 60.
h Ps. 34. 19.
i Mat. 10. 19.
Ac. 23. 11.
k Ps. 22. 21.
l 2 Th. 2. 11.
m Ps. 121. 7.
n chap. 1. 13.
o John 5. 39.
p 2 Pe. 1. 21.
q Ro. 15. 4.
r Ps. 119. 98.
100.
μ or, *perfected*.
s 1 Ti. 5. 21.
6. 13.
v Cæsar Nero,
or, *the Emperor Nero*.

judge the quick and the dead at his appearing and his kingdom;

2 Preach the word; be instant in season, out of season; reprove, rebuke, exhort, with all longsuffering and doctrine.

3 For the time will come when they will not endure sound doctrine; but after their own lusts shall they heap to themselves teachers, having itching ears;

4 And they shall turn away *their* ears from the truth, and shall be turned unto fables.

5 But watch thou in all things, endure afflictions, do the work of an evangelist, make full proof of thy ministry.

6 For I am now ready to be offered, and the time of my departure is at hand.

7 I have fought a good fight, I have finished *my* course, I have kept the faith:

8 Henceforth there is laid up for me a crown of righteousness, which the Lord, the righteous judge, shall give me at that day: and not to me only, but unto all them also that love his appearing.

9 Do thy diligence to come shortly unto me:

10 For Demas hath forsaken me, having loved this present world, and is departed unto Thessalonica; Crescens to Galatia, Titus unto Dalmatia.

11 Only Luke is with me. Take Mark, and bring him with thee; for he is profitable to me for the ministry.

12 And Tychicus have I sent to Ephesus.

13 The cloke that I left at Troas with Carpus, when thou comest bring *with thee*, and the books, *but* especially the parchments.

14 Alexander the coppersmith did me much evil: the Lord reward him according to his works:

15 Of whom be thou ware also; for he hath greatly withstood our words.

16 At my first answer no man stood with me, but all *men* forsook me: *I pray God* that it may not be laid to their charge.

17 Notwithstanding the Lord stood with me, and strengthened me; that by me the preaching might be fully known, and *that* all the Gentiles might hear: and I was delivered out of the mouth of the lion.

18 And the Lord shall deliver me from every evil work, and will preserve me unto his heavenly kingdom: to whom *be* glory for ever and ever. Amen.

19 Salute Prisca and Aquila, and the household of Onesiphorus.

20 Erastus abode at Corinth: but Trophimus have I left at Miletum sick.

21 Do thy diligence to come before winter. Eubulus greeteth thee, and Pudens, and Linus, and Claudia, and all the brethren.

22 The Lord Jesus Christ *be* with thy spirit. Grace *be* with you. Amen.

The second *epistle* unto Timotheus, ordained the first bishop of the church of the Ephesians, was written from Rome, when Paul was brought before Nero the second time.

A page in F.R.H.'s last Bible that she read and studied at the end of her life.

His voyage towards Rome.   THE ACTS, XXVII.   *His shipwreck at Melita.*

Paul^a and certain other prisoners unto *one* named Julius, a centurion of Augustus' band.

2 And entering into a ship of Adramyttium, we launched, meaning to sail by the coasts of Asia; *one* Aristarchus,^f a Macedonian of Thessalonica, being with us.

3 And the next *day* we touched at Sidon. And Julius courteously entreated^i Paul, and gave *him* liberty to go unto his friends to refresh himself.

4 And when we had launched from thence, we sailed under Cyprus, because the winds were contrary. *See c. 24. l. n.*

5 And when we had sailed over the sea of Cilicia and Pamphylia, we came to Myra, *a city of* Lycia.

6 And there the centurion found a ship of Alexandria sailing into Italy; and he put us therein.

7 And when we had sailed slowly many days, and scarce were come over against Cnidus, the wind not suffering us, we sailed under β Crete, over against Salmone;

8 And, hardly passing it, came unto a place which is called The fair havens; nigh whereunto was the city of Lasea.

9 Now when much time was spent, and when sailing was now dangerous, because the γ fast was now already past, Paul admonished *them,*

10 And said unto them, Sirs, I per-

23 For there stood by me this night^b the angel^c of God, whose^d I am, and whom I serve,

24 Saying, Fear not, Paul; thou must be brought before Cæsar: and, lo, God hath given thee^g all them that sail with thee.

25 Wherefore, sirs, be of good cheer; for I^h believe God, that it shall be even as it was told me.

26 Howbeit, we must be cast upon a certain island.^k

27 But when the fourteenth night was come, as we were driven up and down in Adria, about midnight the shipmen deemed that they drew near to some country;

28 And sounded, and found *it* twenty fathoms: and when they had gone a little further, they sounded again, and found *it* fifteen fathoms.

29 Then fearing lest they should have fallen upon rocks, they cast four anchors out of the stern, and wished^l for the day.

30 And as the shipmen were about to flee out of the ship, when they had let down the boat into the sea, under colour as though they would have cast anchors out of the foreship,

31 Paul said to the centurion and to the soldiers, Except these abide in the ship, ye cannot be saved.

32 Then the soldiers cut off the ropes of the boat, and let her fall off.

A.D. 62.

a ch.25.12,25.
b chap.23.11.
c He. 1.14.
d De. 32.9.
 Ps. 135.4.
 Is. 44.5.
 Mal. 3.17.
 Jno.17. 9,10
 1 Co. 6. 20.
 1 Pe.2.9,10.
e Ps. 116.16.
 Is. 44. 21.
 Da. 3. 17.
f John 12. 26.
 Ro. 1. 9.
 2 Ti. 1. 3.
g Ge.19.21,29
h Lu. 1. 45.
 Ro.4.20,21.
 2 Ti. 1.12.
i chap.24.23.
 28.16.
k chap. 28.1.
l Ps. 130. 6.
β or, *Candy.*
γ The Fast was on the tenth day of

This is part of a page in F.R.H.'s last study Bible, that she read, searched, and marked at the end of her life. "For the mouth of the Lord hath spoken it." Isaiah 40:5 and 58:14. "...hath be said, shall be not do it?" Numbers 23:19 Jesus Christ is the faithful and true witness. Revelation 3:14 "Wherefore, sirs, be of good cheer; for I believe God, that it shall be even as it was told me." Acts 27:25

MORNING STARS;

OR,

NAMES OF CHRIST FOR HIS LITTLE ONES.

BY

FRANCES RIDLEY HAVERGAL.

FORTIETH THOUSAND.

LONDON:
JAMES NISBET & CO.
1881.

CONTENTS.

PREFATORY NOTE.

J UST a week before my dear sister F. R. H. died, I took her letters upstairs. Her pretty kittens Trot and Dot were playing on her bed. She was too ill to care about her letters, but was so pleased to get the first page of *this* book. She looked at it carefully, and with her pencil corrected mistakes. Then she was anxious every reader should have space to add the verses, and asked me to write about it. May I say that she hoped you would read one chapter daily! My dear sister intended writing another book for you, "Evening Stars; or, Promises for the Little Ones." But, though she is gone, the Promises are left. Will you not search them out in your Bibles every evening and just say, as she often did, "This promise is so bright, and it is for me."

MARIA V. G. HAVERGAL.

September, 1879.

PREFACE.

To the Readers of "Little Pillows," "Morning Bells," *and* "Bruey."

WRITING to you does not seem the least like writing an ordinary preface, all stiff and proper; for so many of you have written to ask me to write you another book, and so many loving messages have reached me from others, that we seem to be "friends," don't we? So this comes to you at last, with my love, and many a prayer that it may lead you to look oftener and more steadily at Jesus, the Bright and Morning Star.

One thing I want you very much to be quite clear about. No amount of "good little books" will do you any good unless they lead you to love the Book of books. If you really love Jesus you are quite sure to love His word. But one reason why some of you do not love it half as much as you wish you did, is because you do not know enough of it, and you only *read*; you don't "*search*"; which is what God expressly tells you to do. A capital piece of advice was given by a man who did a very great deal towards leading people to love and know their Bibles. He said. "When you take your Bibles, you should be always hunting for something!" So I have given you something to hunt for every day. You will see that nearly every time I have quoted a text I only tell the chapter where it is to be found, and leave a little blank space for the verse. Now, not one of you is to consider your copy of the book complete till you have found out all these verses and put them in yourself with a nice fine pen or sharp pencil! So, you see, I have left *you* to finish the book, and thus given you each "something to do" and something to hunt for, which I hope will be only a beginning of your hunting for a great deal more. Every verse that you find I should like you *also* to mark in your own Bibles; then you will find them again much more easily, and be often reminded of them in time to come.

Though you will find here thirty-one names of the Lord Jesus Christ, you must not think these are nearly all. Some I had written about before, such as "My King," "Our Surety," and others, and the rest had to be left out for want of room. But this is something else to be hunted for. Find out all the rest, and write them at the end of this book. And then, not till then, you may write "*Finis!*"

Frances Ridley Havergal.

MORNING STARS.

1.

Our Saviour.

"The Father sent the Son to be the Saviour of the world."—1 John 4:   .

WE must begin with this. For until we know the Lord Jesus as our Saviour, we cannot really know Him as anything else.

If you were drowning, it would be no use to call out to you about a kind friend who was ready to do all sorts of things for you. The first thing he would do for you would be to jump in and save you. So Jesus must be your Saviour first, and then all His other names will be precious and beautiful to you.

Perhaps you have heard the Lord Jesus spoken of as Friend, or Shepherd, or Master, and have thought how nice it would be if you could call Him so for yourself. And may be you wondered why the names which made others so glad did not seem to bring any gladness to you. This is because you had not begun at the beginning. And the beginning is the great fact that we are sinners, and cannot do without a Saviour. It does not matter how old or how young anybody is, God says "*all* have sinned," and "there is no difference" (Romans 3:   ). Not a bit of difference in His sight between you and a poor little untaught gutter child! Both are real sinners, and cannot be saved without a real Saviour; and Jesus is ready to save him and to save you, both alike. Some people will tell you you are better than they, because you have been brought up as a little Christian. But St. Paul himself said: "What then? Are we better than they? No; in no wise" (Romans 3:   ). And surely, if St. Paul wanted a Saviour, you and I must want one. Jesus says He did not come to call the righteous (Matthew 9:   ); but He says, "The Son of Man is come to seek and to save that which was lost" (Luke 19:   ); and "Christ Jesus came into the world to save sinners" (1 Timothy 1:   ).

So you see, Jesus did not come to have anything to do with us unless we own to being "lost" and "sinners." But if you say, "Yes, I am a sinner, and I am like the prodigal son, lost, and far away," then you are just the one that Jesus came to save. And then you may say, "Lord, save me" (Matthew 14:　); because you know you want saving. And then Jesus saves you surely and certainly, else He would not be a Saviour; for He is a Saviour because He saves, and this is what His very name means (Matthew 1:　). He is "a Saviour, and a great one" (Isaiah 19:　). He is "mighty to save" (Isaiah 63:　). And as soon as you come to Him for the salvation you want, you will say, "The Lord was ready to save *Me*" (Isaiah 38:　).

I must give you some verses written by a little girl named Alice, only eleven years old. You will see how she came to Jesus as her Saviour, and found this precious name true for herself. Come! and you will find it true for you, for He is "Jesus Christ, the *same* yesterday, and to-day, and forever" (Hebrews 13:　).

> One day I was in trouble,
>   And my heart was sore distressed;
> But Jesus came to me and said,
>   "Come, and I will give you rest."
>
> I went to Him, and told Him
>   I'd a debt I could not pay;
> He said to me, "Dost thou not know
>   My blood washed it away?"
>
> He took and laid me in His arms,
>   With my head upon His breast,
> And now I'm with my Saviour,
>   I'm quiet and at rest.
>
> I pray each day and every night,
>   Dear friends, that all of you
> May trust the loving Saviour,
>   And be made happy too.

2.

The Bright and Morning Star.

"I am ... the Bright and Morning Star."—Revelation 22:   .

THIS name of the Lord Jesus seems as if it must be meant especially for children, for it is those who get up early who see the beautiful morning star, shining in the quiet sky that is just beginning to be touched with a promise of dawn, and He says, "they that seek Me early shall find Me" (Proverbs 8:   ). A star shines out in the dark sky and the darkness cannot put it out, but only makes it all the brighter. So if we look up to Jesus as our Star, even if there seems nothing else to make us happy, and nothing to be seen but some dark trouble all around He will shine in our hearts (2 Corinthians 4:   ); and we shall have light and gladness in them (Psalm 4:   ).

A star is always true. If we were going in a wrong direction across a wide moor, directly we caught sight of a star that we knew, we should be shown our mistake. So when we think of Jesus we shall see whether we are going right or wrong, whether we are following Him or going away from Him. When we stop and say to ourselves, "what would Jesus do?" it is like looking up at the star to see which way to go.

Jesus calls Himself the Bright Star, for He is the Brightness of the Father's glory (Hebrews 1:   ). Nothing makes anyone look so bright as looking at His brightness and beauty. You could not possibly have a dismal face while you are really "looking unto Jesus" (Hebrews 12:   ), any more than a little mirror would look dark if you held it up to catch the rays of a bright light.

He calls Himself the Morning Star too, because when we see that shining clear and still we know that the darkness is passing, and very soon the day will break and the shadows flee away (Song of Solomon 2:   ). The sight of the morning star is the promise of the day. And so if you get a little glimpse by faith of the brightness of the Lord Jesus Christ now, it is only a beginning of clearer sight, and a pledge of the glorious day that has no night, in the land where you shall see the King in His beauty (Isaiah 33:   ).

3.

Our Friend.

"This is my Friend."—Song of Solomon 5:   .

ONLY think of this! Think of the Lord Jesus Himself, whom all the angels of God worship (Hebrews 1:   ), the King of kings, full of glory and beauty, letting you look up to Him and say, "This is my Friend!" May you really? Yes, *really*; for Jesus says, "I have called you friends" (John 15:   ).

It is so nice to have a real friend. Don't you feel as if you would do anything for your particular friend? Don't you look forward to being together and telling each other everything? Does it not make it a delightful day if your friend is coming? But "what a Friend we have in Jesus!" A much more real friend than anyone else! He loves you a great deal more, and thinks a great deal more about you, than the very dearest friend you ever had. He does not come just now and then, and leave you alone between whiles; but He is like a friend that always stays with us, so that any minute we may talk to Him and be happy with Him. Never any "good-bye" in this wonderful friendship! (Hebrews 13:   ).

He is such a patient Friend. How very often we grieve Him, and do or say something that we know He would not like, and forget that He is there all the time! (Matthew 28:   ). And still He is our Friend, and forgives us, and goes on loving us.

He is such a kind Friend. Has He not been kind to you, now? Just think what you would do if He had not given you all the little mercies as well as the great ones around you! (Isaiah 63:   ). See how He thinks of everything for you, so that they are new every morning (Lamentations 3:   ).

He is such a wise Friend. He never makes a mistake in anything He sends you or bids you do; even if you do not see at all why He lets something come that you do not like, you may be quite sure He is quite right.

He must be the most loving Friend, because He died for you. He says, "greater love hath no man than this, that a man lay down his life for his friends" (John 15:   ). *That* is what He did for you. Can you see it? Look at your Saviour crucified upon the cross, crowned with the sharp thorns, bleeding and suffering unto death for you. Is it not wonderful that you may say, "This is *my* Friend?"

4.

Our Brother.

"He is not ashamed to call them brethren."—Hebrews 2:   .

SOMETIMES people do not like it to be known if they have relations not so well off as themselves, and do not care to mention them. How different this is from the Lord Jesus. He is the Son of God, the King of kings, and yet He is not ashamed to call us brethren. He came down to earth on purpose to be made like us in everything (Hebrews 2:   ), so that He might be our brother. He is our good, kind, strong Elder Brother, and He will be to us everything you can think of about the very best brother you ever heard of.

What a difference it makes to the summer holidays when a dear elder brother comes home! And if a great home trouble comes, who is wanted so much as the elder brother who feels it all because it is his sorrow too, and yet knows what to do and how to help the others through the dark time? So it is Jesus who can make all your happiest times happier still, and yet He is the Brother born for adversity (Proverbs 17:   ), who comes to comfort and help us as no one else can, when we are in trouble.

Perhaps you think, "Oh, how I should like to know that Jesus is *my* Brother!" If He is your Saviour, He will be to you all that every one of His other beautiful names tells you He is. But He has told us something which should help you to lay hold of this one. When the multitude sat about Him, listening to His words (Mark 3:   ), He looked round about on them and said, "Behold My mother and My brethren! For whosoever shall do the will of God, the same is My brother, and My sister, and My mother." Doing the will of God is just trying to do what He tells you and what pleases Him. And Jesus knows if you are really wishing and trying to do this. And if you are, that shows you are His little brother or His little sister, for He says so. And although He is the Mighty God, He is not ashamed to call you so, and you may say:

> Christ is my Father and my Friend,
> My Brother and my Love;
> My Head, my Hope, my Counsellor.
> My Advocate above.

5.

Our Redeemer.

"I know that my Redeemer liveth."—Job 19:   .

REDEEMING means buying back something that has been sold or fallen into the power of an enemy. When Adam and Eve disobeyed God and obeyed the devil, it was like selling themselves to him to be his servants instead of God's. For it says, "Know ye not that to whom ye yield yourselves servants to obey, his servants ye are to whom ye obey?" (Romans 6:   ). And so all their children were sold too, "sold under sin" (Romans 7:   ); and every one of them, you and I as well as the rest, have done the same thing, disobeyed God. God says to us all, "Ye have sold yourselves for nought" (Isaiah 52:   ). We could never redeem our souls ourselves, for we have nothing to do it with. And no one can do it for us (Psalm 49:   ); all the silver and gold in the world would not be enough to redeem only one soul. Nothing but Jesus Christ's own blood could do it (1 Peter 1:   ). He saw that there was no one else to do it (Isaiah 59:   ), and so "in His love and in His pity He redeemed us" (Isaiah 63:   ). That is, He gave His own blood as the price of buying us back from Satan, taking us out of his service and out of his power, and buying us to be God's own children and His own happy little servants. And now He says to you, "Ye are not your own, for ye are bought with a price" (1 Corinthians 6:   ). How we ought to thank Him for this! You see it is not something that we *hope* He will do for us, but something that He really *has done* for us and that can never be undone. And so even now we ought to echo the song of the saints around the throne, and say, "Thou wast slain, and hast redeemed us to God by Thy blood" (Revelation 5:   ). He means us to know that He is our Redeemer for He says, "thou shalt know that I the Lord am thy Saviour and thy Redeemer" (Isaiah 60:   ). When you are quite sure a thing is true, you say "I know." You are quite sure it is true that Jesus has redeemed us, because God's word tells us so in a great many places (Ephesians 1:   ; Hebrews 9:   ; Luke 1:   ); and you are quite sure that He has risen from the dead and is "alive for evermore" (Revelation 1:   ), and so you may say without fear, "I *know* that my Redeemer liveth." And the Lord Jesus answers, "Fear not, for I have redeemed thee; thou art Mine" (Isaiah 43:   ).

I could not do without Thee,
   O Saviour of the lost!
Whose wondrous love redeemed me
   At such tremendous cost.
Thy righteousness, Thy pardon,
   Thy precious blood must be
My only hope and comfort,
   My glory and my plea!

6.

Our Master.

"Jesus saith unto her, Mary. She turned herself and saith unto Him, Rabboni; which is to say Master."—John 20:   .

I SHOULD think no one ever could have been happier than Mary was that moment when she said "Master!" But every one who says "Master," and *means it,* must be happy too; for we do not care to call Jesus "Master" until we love Him, and loving Him always makes people happy.

When we have learnt the sweet words "my Saviour" and "my Redeemer," because we believe that Jesus has saved us and bought us with His precious blood, then we are sure to want to call Him "my Master." "I want to do something for Jesus" is one of the first wishes that rises up in our hearts when we see what He has done for us, and perhaps it is one of the surest proofs that we do love Him. We feel like the Queen of Sheba when she said, "Happy are these thy servants" (1 Kings 10:   ). And when we have tried a little bit of His service we are very glad to say, "O Lord, truly I am Thy servant" (Psalm 116:   ).

But it is the Master Himself that makes the service sweet, and so we are gladder still when we just look up to Him and say, like Mary, "Master!" When we say that word to Him it makes it all so real. For we have not only to look back at a dying Saviour, but to look up at a living one. When Mary said it, He had come up out of the tomb never to die any more (Romans 6:   ), but always to live for us; and when we call Him by that name it may remind us that He is risen, and is really alive now, and that He says, "because I live ye shall live also" (John 14:   ).

He has given a beautiful answer to every one who loves Him enough to call Him by this name. He says, "Ye call Me Master and Lord, and ye say well" (John 13:   ). So He likes to hear us say it, and values the love of the poor little sinful heart that yet looks up and says, "I love my Master" (Exodus 21:   ).

I love, I love my Master,
    I will not go out free!
He loves me, oh, so lovingly,
    He is so good to me!

I love, I love my Master,
    He shed His blood for me,
To ransom me from Satan's power,

From sin's hard slavery.

I love, I love my Master,
    Oh, how He worked for me!
He worked out God's salvation,
    So great, so full, so free.

My Master, O my Master,
    If I may work for Thee,
And tell out Thy salvation,
    How happy shall I be!

ELLEN P. SHAW.

For He hath met my longing
    With word of golden tone,
That I shall serve for ever
    Himself, Himself alone.

"Shall serve Him," and "for ever:"
    O hope most sure, most fair!
The perfect love outpouring
    In perfect service there!

Rejoicing and adoring,
    Henceforth my song shall be:
I love, I love my Master,
    I will not go out free!

F. R. H.

Note: These three last verses are added since their writer went away to "serve Him day and night in His temple."

7.

Our Physician.

"They that be whole need not a physician, but they that are sick."—Matthew 9:   .

HOW is it that some people care so very much about these beautiful names of Christ, and others do not care at all about them? It just depends upon whether the Holy Spirit has opened our eyes to see that we are in want of exactly the very thing that Jesus is called. That is what makes all the difference.

People who think they have nothing the matter with them do not wish for a doctor. If you heard that there was a wonderful man come to the neighbourhood who could cure consumption, I don't suppose you would think twice about it, you who have good strong lungs, and can run, and sing, and laugh! But if you had a dreadful cough, and had seen people shake their heads and whisper, "Ah, poor child, I'm afraid it is consumption!" you would want to hear everything you could about this doctor; and when they kept telling you how clever he was and how many people he had cured, I think you would want very much to go to him and be cured too.

Now everyone of us is born into the world with a disease in our souls called sin (Romans 3:   ); "and sin, when it is finished, bringeth forth death" (James 1:   ). And the very worst sign of this disease is when we do not feel it, and do not know that we have it (Revelation 3:   ).

There is only One who can heal us, and if He does not heal us we never can be healed at all (Acts 4:   ); that is Jesus, the Good Physician; and as He never sent anyone away without healing who came to Him on earth (Matthew 12:   ), so He never sends away anyone (John 6:   ) who comes to Him now to be healed of the plague of sin. He "healeth all thy diseases" (Psalm 103:   ).

It is a great step toward healing when we are shown that we do want the Physician. Then we may come at once to Him, no matter at all how bad we feel, and say, "Heal my soul, for I have sinned against Thee" (Psalm 41:   ); and then He says, "I am the Lord that healeth thee" (Exodus 15:   ).

But suppose you do not feel so very bad as all that, what then? Well, then you must just believe that God knows better than you, and that you *are* a sinner and need healing, although you don't feel it. And then you must not wait to feel your sinfulness; if you do Satan will be very clever in contriving to hide it from you, so that you may not come to Jesus at all. So don't wait for that, nor for anything, but come and tell the Lord Jesus that, though you do not yet *feel* much about it, yet you *know* you need to be saved and healed, and ask Him to be your Good Physician, and to undertake your case just as you are; and then you may say, "Heal me, O Lord, and I shall be healed" (Jeremiah 17:	); for "with His stripes we are healed" (Isaiah 53:	).

8.

Our Substitute.

"Christ also hath once suffered for sins, the Just for the unjust, that He might bring us to God."—1 Peter 3:	.

WE do not find the word "substitute" in the Bible, but the sense of it comes over and over again. It means one person put in another person's place, or one thing put instead of another.

There was a little girl of three years old, who showed that she understood perfectly about the Lord Jesus being our Substitute. She put her little hands together and said, "I thank You, Jesus, that You was punished instead of me!" That is it! the Lord Jesus taking our place, and punished instead of us. That was why He suffered; He was the Just One, that is, perfectly good; and we are the unjust, that is, sinful and bad; and so He suffered for our sins, the Just One suffering instead of us, the unjust ones.

There are many pictures of this in the Bible. One is when Judah, the elder brother, wanted to save Benjamin from being kept as a slave in Egypt. He begged hard that he might take his brother's place, and stay "instead of the lad" (Genesis 44:	). That was offering to be his substitute. When an Israelite had sinned he was to bring a clean animal to be killed and offered for him; and when he put his hand on the head of the burnt-offering it was "accepted for him" (Leviticus 1:	). That was to teach him that Some One must suffer and shed blood for his sin, and that His death would be accepted instead of his being punished.

The Lord Jesus was wounded for our transgressions, and was bruised for our iniquities; that is, He was wounded and bruised *instead* of our being punished for them (Isaiah 53:	). And because we were like sheep going astray Jesus was led like a sheep to the slaughter, instead, always instead, of us! Dear children, when you hear or read the story of the cross, think of this, that Jesus was your Substitute as He hung there in all that agony; He bore it all for love of you, and for your sins, and *instead of* you!

Oh, think of His sorrow!
That we may know
His wondrous love
In His wondrous woe.

9.

Our Shepherd.

"Our Lord Jesus, that great Shepherd of the sheep."—Hebrews 13:   .

HERE is a little lesson for you, all in threes. Jesus Christ is the Good Shepherd, and the Great Shepherd, and the Chief Shepherd. And these three names tell us of His death, His resurrection, and His ascension.

For, as the Good Shepherd He laid down His life for the sheep (John 10:   ); as the Great Shepherd He was brought again from the dead (Hebrews 13:   ); and as the Chief Shepherd He is now gone up on high, and shall appear when He comes again (1 Peter 5:   ).

He laid down His life that He might give us a crown of life (Revelation 2:   ). He was raised that we might be justified (Romans 4:   ), that is, accounted righteous before God, so that He might give us the crown of righteousness (2 Timothy 4:   ); and He is coming again to give us a crown of glory that fadeth not away (1 Peter 5:   ). So the three promised crowns seem linked with these three beautiful names of Jesus, who is both our Shepherd and our King.

And now think a little about what "Shepherd" means for *you*. It means that you have Some One to belong to, that you are not your own (1 Corinthians 6:   ).

It means that you have Some One to take care of you, Some One who will watch you and will not let you get lost (Luke 15:   ).

It means that you have Some One who feeds you and will not let you starve, and if you keep near Him He will not let you be hungry at all (Ezekiel 34:   ).

It means that you have Some One who knows you and calls you by name (John 10:   ).

It means that this One loves you so much that He laid down His life for you (ver.   ).

It means that He came on purpose to give you life, and life more abundantly (ver.   ), that is, that you should not be a just-alive sort of Christian, but a strong, bright, happy one, as full of life as the lambs look when they are bounding about on a sunny May morning.

And it means that He will not let anyone pluck you out of His hand, and that He has given His promise that you shall never perish (ver.   ).

Now what can you want more? Should you not say, "the Lord is my Shepherd, I shall not want" (Psalm 23:   ); and will you not sing—

> To praise our Shepherd's care,
>   His wisdom, love, and might,
> Your loudest, loftiest songs prepare,
>   And bid the world unite.
>
> Supremely good and great,
>   He tends His blood-bought fold;
> He stoops, though throned in highest state,
>   The feeblest to uphold.
>
> He hears their softest plaint,
>   He sees them when they roam;
> And if His meanest lamb should faint,
>   His bosom bears it home.

Rev. W. H. Havergal.

10.

Our Passover.

"Christ our Passover is sacrificed for us."—1 Corinthians 5:   .

THAT was a terrible night when the last of the ten plagues fell upon Pharaoh and his land. How would you have felt if you had been one of the first-born, and had heard Moses proclaim that about midnight the Lord would go out (Exodus 11:   ), and all the firstborn in Egypt should die! Would you not have made haste to ask if there was not some way to escape being smitten? And would you not have been very glad and comforted to hear that there was a way by which you might be quite safe?

It seemed a very strange way. A lamb was to be killed and eaten that evening, and the blood was to be sprinkled on the door posts. And God said: "When I see the blood I will pass over you" (Exodus 12:   ). People might have said: "But we don't understand! *why* shall we be safe inside when the blood is sprinkled?" Their not understanding did not matter at all; God had said it, and that was enough. Those that believed His word and took shelter under it were safe from the Destroyer; but as for all the Egyptians who had no blood sprinkled, "there was not a house where there was not one dead."

God does not say now, "the firstborn shall die," but He says, "the soul that sinneth, it shall die" (Ezekiel 18:   ). And have not you and I sinned? But Christ our Passover is sacrificed for us. So He says, "Behold the Lamb of God which taketh away the sin of the world" (John 1:   ). By His own blood (Hebrews 9:   ), as of a lamb (1 Peter 1:   ), He has obtained redemption and salvation for us. Nothing else can wash away our sins (Hebrews 9:   ; Revelation 1:   ), so nothing else could save us. This holy Lamb of God has been slain; that was done long ago, and now we have only to take shelter under His precious blood, believing what God says about it, and we are safe. We do not have to wait till we can quite understand about it, and God does not wait for *us* to see; but He says, "when *I* see the blood I will pass over you." No destroyer shall touch the soul that believes God's word about Jesus and His precious blood, and takes shelter under that.

11.

Our Intercessor.

"It is Christ that died, yea rather, that is risen again, who is even at the right hand of God, who also maketh intercession for us."—Romans 8: .

HERE are four wonderful steps, rising one above another. As we stand on each one we see more and more reason for happy confidence in our Lord Jesus Christ. The first is that He died for us. But if He had remained in the grave we could never have known that God had accepted His great atonement for us. So the next step of confidence is that He is risen again, so that He is our living Saviour who says, "Because I live, ye shall live also" (John 14:). The next is that He is even at the right hand of God, in all His power and glory, preparing a place for us, and by His Spirit preparing us for it.

Jesus dying, risen, and gone up to heaven, all for us! What could we think of more? Yet His wonderful love goes farther still, for He "also maketh intercession for us." That means, He is praying for us. One would have thought that when He went back to heaven, after all His suffering for us on earth, He would have done enough for us, and would have something else to do than be thinking about us any more. But as long as one of His dear children lives on earth, He will go on praying for each one to the end, even as He loves each one to the end (John 13:); for "He *ever* liveth to make intercession for us" (Hebrews 7:).

Think now, Jesus is praying for you to-day! Perhaps you have thought very little about Him, and grieved His loving heart, and only said a few words of cold prayers without really praying to Him at all; and He has been praying for you all the time!

Would you like to know for certain that He prays for *you?* Then see what He says in that beautiful last prayer of His on earth: "neither pray I for these alone, but for all them which shall believe on Me through their word" (John 17:). So if you are, "one of these little ones which believe in Me" (Matthew 18:), Jesus prays for you as certainly as He did for Peter when He said, "I have prayed for thee" (Luke 22:).

12.

The Unspeakable Gift.

"Thanks be unto God for His unspeakable Gift."—2 Corinthians 9:   .

"THE things which are freely given to us of God" are so many and so great that we cannot know them all unless He gives us the Holy Spirit to make us know them (1 Corinthians 2:   ). Once two young friends of mine set to work to make a list of all God's gifts mentioned in the Bible. They found 530 gifts, and wrote them out in a scroll, and it was more than two yards long in three columns, and in small writing too! Suppose you try and make a list at least one yard long!

What will you put down as the best gift of all? Here is the answer:

"God so loved the world, that *He gave His only begotten Son,* that whosoever believeth in Him should not perish, but have everlasting life" (John 3:   ).

All the other good gifts from our Father (James 1:   ) come through this first great Gift, Jesus Himself. For He received gifts for us (Psalm 68:   ), and now He is sending them down to us, daily loading us with benefits (ver.   ).

Unless we are very careless and ungrateful indeed, we always care about a gift. "A gift is as a precious stone in the eyes of him that hath it" (Proverbs 17:   ). Oh, what must God think of those who do not care about the most precious Gift He could possibly have given us! Dear ones, have *you* cared for this wonderful Gift? Have *you* ever thanked God for giving you His own dear Son? Think of His having given you Jesus to be to you all that these beautiful names describe. Think how He did not merely give Him, but "gave Him up for us all" (Romans 8:   ). Gave Him up all the thirty-three long years, gave Him up to be scourged and crucified! What would anyone think of you if they gave you a magnificent present, that cost them a very great deal to part with, and you never said "Thank you!" Oh, what must God think if you do not thank Him for giving the Son of His love!

But if you do thank Him, what does that show? What does it show when you say, "Oh, thank you very much!" for a birthday present? Does it not show the giver that you believe it is meant for you, and that you have taken it for your own? And then he leaves it with you, and it *is* your own. Is there a little faint heart who is saying, "Oh, I *should* like to know that Jesus is mine?" He is God's gift to every one who will accept Him; so now you just go and kneel alone before God, and thank Him for His unspeakable Gift; and that will show that you have accepted Him, and that He *is* yours.

I gave My life for thee,
   My precious blood I shed
That thou might'st ransomed be
   And quickened from the dead.
I gave My life for thee:
What hast thou given for Me?

13.

Our Leader.

"Behold I have given Him for a witness to the people, a Leader and commander to the people."—Isaiah 55:   .

OUR Heavenly Father knew that we could never find our way to heaven by ourselves. He knew, too, that we should never find even a little bit of the right way for ourselves. So He gave us a Leader. It would have been a great deal if He had sent an angel to lead us; but in His great love to us He did much more than that, He sent Jesus down to us and said, "Behold, I have given *Him* for a Leader."

Those who want to get to the top of very high mountains in Switzerland are anxious to have the very best guide they can hear of. Very often they write to a first-rate guide months beforehand to make sure, and he engages himself, so that when they come to begin their climb the guide is all ready for them. Now we did not engage our heavenly Guide, but God knew how much we should need Him. So He engaged the Lord Jesus to be our Leader ages before we were born. And so, now that you are, I hope, beginning the upward path, Jesus is there, keeping God's promise, and ready to be your Leader.

We want inside leading and outside leading, and Jesus does both. The inside leading comes first, for He leads us to God as our Father. If He did not we never should come near at all, but always be far off, for He says, "no man cometh unto the Father but by Me" (John 14:   ). Then He leads us in the way of righteousness (Proverbs 8:   ), that is, He leads us to do what is right. He does not only lead all His people in general like a flock (Psalm 80:   ), but He calls each of us by name and leads us (John 10:   ). So you may say, like David, "He leadeth *me*" (Psalm 23:   ).

Then there is the outside leading, sometimes leading you to very pleasant places (Psalm 16:   ), and sometimes leading you where you do not like to go. But if Jesus really is your Leader He will always lead you by the right way (Psalm 107:   ). He never makes a mistake in arranging for His children. He leads gently as well as rightly, like Jacob, who said he would lead on softly, according as the children should be able to endure (Genesis 33:   ). And He always leads safely (Psalm 78:   ); so that we need not fear.

He Himself was led as a sheep to the slaughter (Acts 8:   ). So He knows how to lead His lambs till He brings them safe to heaven. And still He will be their Leader, for the Lamb which is in the midst of the throne shall feed them, and lead them unto living fountains of waters, and God shall wipe away all tears from their eyes (Revelation 7:   ).

Jesus, loving Saviour,
Only Thou dost know
All that may befall us
As we onward go.
So we humbly pray Thee
Take us by the hand,
Lead us ever upward
To the Better Land.

14.

Our Commander.

"Behold, I have given Him for a witness to the people, a leader and Commander to the people."—Isaiah 55:   .

IF Jesus is our Leader, He must be our Commander too.

When God meant to bring the Israelites into the promised land He set Joshua over them to lead them out and bring them in (Numbers 27:   ); and when Joshua was made their leader the people said, "All that thou commandest us we will do" (Joshua 1:   ).

Are you ready to say that to the Lord Jesus? Does it seem very hard? Are you afraid He may command you something you would not like to do? It would be not only very hard, but quite impossible, to do what He commands, if it were not for two things.

The first is, that He has promised to write His laws in our hearts (Hebrews 8:   ); which means that He will make our hearts willing and glad to keep them. And He gives His Holy Spirit to enable us to keep them.

And the second is, that love makes all the difference to obedience. When sailors have a good commander of their ship they like doing what he wants done. The hardship to them would be to be prevented from doing it. So, if we love our Commander, we shall *want* to do what He bids us. Suppose you had been there that last, sweet, solemn evening, when He had the last long talk with His disciples, just before He went to Gethsemane, and had heard Him say, "If ye love Me, keep My commandments" (John 14:   ), don't you think you would have wished to keep them? Would you have thought it hard then?

Look in those beautiful chapters (John 14:   , and 15:   ), and find out for yourself what Jesus promises to those who keep His commandments; and then see what St. John says about them in his First Epistle (chap. 5:   ); for, after all, He never commands us one single thing but what will make us happy if we only do *exactly* what He tells us. They are "for our good, always" (Deuteronomy 6:   ). If everybody kept them, everybody would be happy, as happy as the angels (Psalm 103:   ); for "blessed" (that means very happy *indeed*) "is the man that delighteth greatly in His commandments" (Psalm 112:   ). Ask Him to make you love Him so much that you may say, "I will delight myself in Thy commandments, which I have loved" (Psalm 119:   ).

Just to ask Him what to do
　　All the day,
And to make you quick and true
　　To obey.
Just to know the needed grace
　　He bestoweth,
Every bar of time and place
　　Overfloweth.
Just to take thy orders straight
　　From the Master's own command.
Blessèd day! when thus we wait
　　Always at our Sovereign's hand.

15.

Our Head.

"The Head, even Christ."—Ephesians 4:   .

HERE is another name of Christ as the Gift of God; for God "gave Him to be Head over all things to the Church, which is His body" (Ephesians 1:   ). Perhaps you never thought before of Jesus being your Head! But you will find great help in thinking about everything that God has told us about Him.

If He is our Head, and we are His body, it is very plain that we cannot do without Him. What could your hands and feet do if they were not joined to your head? so the Lord Jesus might well say, "without Me ye can do nothing" (John 15:   ).

If He is our Head, you cannot grow without Him; and more than that, you cannot live without Him, any more than you could if your head were cut off. There is only death in the soul that is without Jesus, no real life at all: for "he that hath the Son hath life; and he that hath not the Son of God hath not life" (1 John 5:   ).

I said you could not grow without Him. That is why some of you do not seem to grow better and brighter and stronger little Christians; it is when you are "not holding the Head" (Colossians 2:   ), (that is, not keeping close to Jesus) that you do not get on. He does not want you to be like a poor little cripple or dwarf, but to grow up into Him in all things (Ephesians 4:   ).

> Let me then be always growing,
> Never, never standing still;
> Listening, learning, better knowing
> Thee and Thy most holy will.

If Jesus is your Head, then you are the body of Christ, and members in particular (1 Corinthians 12:   ). Yes, each of you "*in particular*"; not everybody in general! And even if you are a very little member, or a very feeble member (ver.   ), you are "necessary," and Jesus would not do without you, any more than your head would choose to do without one of your fingers or feet. Fancy your saying, "Oh, I don't care much about this foot; you may cut it off if you like!" Just so the Lord Jesus cares about every little member who is joined to Him, and will not let it be cut off from His body; the Head cannot say to the feet, I have no need of you (ver.   ). Now is it not a very precious name which teaches us such a precious truth?

Now you will understand better how Jesus feels for us; for if your little finger is hurt, your head does not have to be told! you know about it, and feel it, and cry out, in an instant. So if the least little member of Christ suffers, He knows, and feels, and sympathizes, because "Christ is the Head" (Ephesians 5:   ).

> Make Thy members every hour
>   For Thy blessèd service meet;
> Earnest tongues, and arms of power,
>   Skilful hands, and hastening feet,
> Ever ready to fulfil
> All Thy word, and all Thy will.

16.

Our Light.

"I am the Light of the world; he that followeth Me shall not walk in darkness, but shall have the light of life."—John 8:   .

SOME people don't see what they want with this Light! they think their own eyes and common-sense, and what they call "the light of reason," are quite enough for them. But Jesus says, "Take heed therefore that the light that is in thee be not darkness" (Luke 11:   ); and, "If therefore the light that is in thee be darkness, how great is that darkness!" (Matthew 6:   ). For Jesus Himself is the true Light (John 1:   ), and if we have not the true Light of course we can't see right.

The Holy Spirit very often shows us the darkness first, so as to make us seek the Light. A young girl said to me, "I can't see my way through the sins." It was a great thing that the good Spirit was showing her the darkness. Nothing is worse than not to know that we are "poor, and miserable, and blind" (Revelation 3:   ), because then we do not want the Light. Now if you feel something like that girl, just bring the sins to Jesus, bring the darkness to the Light, and in His light you shall see light (Psalm 36:   ). We *cannot* be in the dark when we come close to a bright light; there cannot be darkness in our hearts when we open the door and let the Lord Jesus come in.

Some of you know well enough already what the difference is, and how true it comes that "Christ shall give thee light" (Ephesians 5:   ). How the puzzles are made clear, and the doubts all go we don't know where, and the shadows flee away, and everything seems bright, when we really come to Jesus! Ever so many of you are saying, I know, as you read this, "Yes, yes! that is just it!" Why not all of you?

This is one of the special things that God gave Jesus to be: "a Light of the Gentiles" (Isaiah 42:   ). Old Simeon was so glad when he saw the Light that he was ready to die at once (Luke 2:   ). There are three names of Jesus in that beautiful little song of Simeon's, "Lord, now lettest Thou." Think about them next time you sing it; and ask Jesus to be your Salvation, your Light, and your Glory. Then, when He lets you depart in peace, "the Lord shall be unto thee an Everlasting Light, and thy God thy Glory" (Isaiah 60:   ).

It was not always light with me; for many a sinful year
I walked in darkness, far from Thee; but Thou hast brought me near,
And washed me in Thy precious blood, and taught me by Thy grace,
And lifted up on my poor soul the brightness of Thy face.

My Saviour died in darkness that I might live in light,
He closed His eyes in death that mine might have the heavenly sight;
He gave up all His glory to bring it down to me,
And took the sinner's place that He the sinner's Friend might be.

His Spirit shines upon His word, and makes it sweet indeed,
Just like a shining lamp held up beside me as I read;
And brings it to my mind again alone upon my bed,
Till all abroad within my heart the love of God is shed.

17.

Our Life.

"When Christ, who is our Life, shall appear, then shall ye also appear with Him in glory."—Colossians 3:   .

ONCE I asked a poor French girl if she was afraid to die. She shrugged her shoulders, and said, "Ah, death, death! it is terrible, terrible!" She was quite right. For death *is* terrible in itself, and the second death (Revelation 20:   ) is more terrible still. And if persons have never felt afraid to die, I am afraid it shows they do not know anything about it, like a child fast asleep in a burning house.

But just because death is terrible Christ our Life is precious. This is good news for every one who is afraid to die. Jesus Christ gives us life, not for trying, not even for asking, but only just for believing on Him! He says, "Verily, verily, I say unto you, He that believeth on Me hath everlasting life" (John 6:   ). Would Jesus have said that, and not mean it? Would He have said that if you believe in Him you have everlasting life, if He only meant that He would perhaps give it you and perhaps not? And would He have said *"everlasting* life," if it was a life that you might lose to-morrow and that might *not* last? Take the gladness of the good news, and believe that Jesus meant what He said, and meant it for you! And then you need not fear death any more than you fear to go to sleep, for death is only falling asleep for those who are safe in Jesus. It will be only like going to sleep in your little bed, and waking up in a different place, the most beautiful place you can imagine!

But Jesus does more than give us life. He *is* our Life. Thinking of Him as our Head will help you to understand this. Your finger, for instance, is not a separate little live thing; it lives because it is joined to your head, and to what a little girl called your "think"; and it is because your head is alive that your finger is alive. Just so Jesus says, "because I live, ye shall live also" (John 14:   ).

And how long will Jesus live? He says, "Behold I am alive for evermore" (Revelation 1:   ). So how long will every little member of Christ live? Must it not be "for evermore" too? So you see the promise of everlasting life is sure because "Christ being raised from the dead dieth no more" (Romans 6:   ). He died for us, that whether we wake or sleep we should live together with Him (1 Thessalonians 5:   ). Do you not see? If you believe in Jesus, your life depends on His life, and it is "hid" with Him (Colossians 3:   ). And do you think Satan could get at what is hid with Christ? Must it not be quite safe there?

Jesus, Thy life is mine!
   Dwell evermore in me!
      And let me see
That nothing can untwine
      My life from Thine.

Jesus, my life is Thine,
   And evermore shall be
      Hidden in Thee!
For nothing can untwine
      Thy life from mine.

18.

Our Rock.

"Lead me to the Rock that is higher than I."—Psalm 61: .

THERE are so many thoughts about Jesus as our Rock, that we can only find room for a very few of them.

First, He is the smitten Rock (Numbers 20:); for He was smitten of God (Isaiah 53:), and smitten of man too, as we read in the solemn story of His sufferings. Smitten, like the rock in the thirsty desert, with a rod; for it says, "they shall smite the Judge of Israel with a rod upon the cheek" (Micah 5:). Smitten that the stream of life might flow forth for you and me.

Secondly, He is the cleft Rock. God said to Moses, "Behold, there is a place by Me, and thou shalt stand upon a rock" (Exodus 33:). And He put him in a cleft of the rock, and covered him with His hand, while His glory passed by. You know how you like to have a place by one you love, and what an honour it is to have a place by some one who is great or noble! So, when God sets our feet upon the Rock (Psalm 40:), it is a place by Him, a happy place, and an honourable place. It is a safe place too, not only safe from the great enemy now; but when the great and terrible day of the Lord comes (Joel 2:), and His glory is more than the unsheltered ones can bear, those in the cleft of the Rock will have nothing to fear.

Thirdly, He is the Higher Rock. When the tide is beginning to come in, it would be no use standing on a rock no higher than yourself. The waves would very soon dash over that, and drown you. But if you climb up to a higher rock, ever so much above your head, the waves can never reach you. No matter how furiously they roll in, you are just as safe as if there was not such a thing as a wave at all! So when God leads you to the Higher Rock, that is, when His grace draws you to come to Jesus (John 6:), you are safe!

Fourthly, He is the strong Rock (Psalm 31:). David knew what it was to dwell in rocks, to be out of the way of Saul (1 Samuel 23:); and so he said, "Be Thou my strong habitation (margin, a rock of habitation), whereunto I may continually resort" (Psalm 71:). That is just what Jesus is, a strong Rock, where we may always go to be safe out of the way of our enemy, Satan.

Fifthly, He is a Rock of offence (1 Peter 2:). It is very sad and solemn to read this, but it is true. Those who do not like to come to Jesus as the Rock of salvation (Deuteronomy 32:) will know some day what its terrible meaning is. But may all my little readers, and older ones too, be like the coneys, so

wise though so feeble, because they make their houses in the rocks (Proverbs
30:    ). Remember that the Lord Jesus calls those who love Him His doves,
that are in the clefts of the rock (Song of Solomon 2:   ). And if you are like
the coneys and the doves in this, then He says to you, "Let the inhabitants of
the Rock sing!" (Isaiah 42:   ).

19.

Our Righteousness.

"This is His name whereby He shall be called, THE LORD OUR RIGHTEOUSNESS."
—Jeremiah 23:   .

THIS is always printed in large capitals in our Bibles. And no wonder, for it is so very important. You see, righteousness is something that we must have, or we cannot go to heaven, any more than you could go to a grand royal entertainment without a proper dress. They would not let you in if you were all in rags, you know that well enough; nobody but a lunatic would attempt to go in that condition.

All our righteousnesses, that is, all the good things we ever did or tried to do, are filthy rags (Isaiah 64:   ). It is no use trying to make them out to be anything cleaner and better; if God says they are filthy rags, they *are* so.

Even these filthy rags do not cover us; the very best "filthy rag" garment that ever anybody tried to make for himself is so full of holes, and is so scanty, that it cannot cover us. God says, "their webs" (that is, what they try to spin and weave for themselves out of their own goodness) "shall not become garments, neither shall they cover themselves with their own works" (Isaiah 59:   ). What will you do without something better?

When the king came in to see the guests, he saw there a man which had not on a wedding garment. He had no excuse, for the king himself provided the garments. So he was to be bound hand and foot, and cast into outer darkness (Matthew 22:   ). You see, he had to have it *on*; the garment was there for him, and he must have known about it, only he did not choose to accept it and put it on. Even so, we must accept "the righteousness of God which is by faith of Jesus Christ unto all and *upon* all them that believe" (Romans 3:   ). For believing God's word about it is putting it on; and then Jesus Christ Himself is made unto us righteousness (1 Corinthians 1:   ). And then you may say, "I will greatly rejoice in the Lord, my soul shall be joyful in my God: for He hath clothed me with the garments of salvation, He hath covered me with the robe of righteousness" (Isaiah 61:   ).

Does this seem rather dry to you? It would not seem dry if you knew you were just going to be called to stand before God, and that you must either stand in filthy rags or in the perfectly beautiful and spotless robe. What if the call came, and found you hesitating whether you would put it on or not! How you would wish then that you knew Jesus to be the Lord your Righteousness! Ask the Holy Spirit now to show you all that He means in this wonderful name, so that you may say, "In the Lord have I righteousness and strength" (Isaiah 45:).

> Your righteousness, as filthy rags,
> Must all relinquished be,
> And only Jesus' precious blood
> Must be your plea.
>
> Fear not to trust His simple word,
> So sweet, so tried, so true!
> Righteous in Him, for evermore:
> Yes, even you!

20.

Our Captain.

"The Captain of their salvation."—Hebrews 2:   .

THE children of Israel had been vexed and oppressed by the Ammonites for eighteen years (Judges 10:   ). They were "sore distressed," and did not know what to do, because the Ammonites were gathered together against them, and they had no one to begin to fight for them (ver.   ). At last they thought of Jephthah, a mighty man of valour, whom they had treated very badly. They sent and said to him, "Come, and be our captain" (Judges 11:   ). But Jephthah said: "Did ye not hate me and expel me out of my father's house? And why are ye come unto me now, when ye are in distress?" That was the very reason why they had come! and so they said, "*Therefore* we turn again to thee now, that thou mayest go with us, and fight against the children of Ammon." Jephthah did not mean not to go, but only to remind them of their unkindness. For he went with them, and fought for them and delivered them.

I wonder whether you have ever yet found out what strong and terrible enemies you have! If persons have never found sin and self and Satan trying to make them do wrong instead of right, and been oppressed and distressed about it, I am afraid they have been fast asleep, or something worse, "dead in trespasses and sins" (Ephesians 2:   ). Just as a dead Israelite would not have felt vexed and oppressed by the Ammonites' tyranny and cruelty; he would have known nothing about it.

But if you have been awake enough to say, "The good that I would I do not; but the evil that I would not, that I do" (Romans 7:   ); then, like the Israelites, you will be glad to hear of One who is the Captain of our salvation. And though you may not have loved Him at all, and have driven the very thought of Him out of your mind, yet He is so forgiving and gracious that, as soon as ever you cry to Him for help, He will come and be your Captain.

A captain in the Queen's army sometimes has to lead his soldiers on to death. But Jesus, our Captain, only leads us on to life and victory. No one can be defeated while really following Him, for He conquers for us and in us, and makes us more than conquerors because He so loves us (Romans 8:   ). He has conquered all our enemies already, so we only have to pursue the defeated foes with the shout of victory. He is the Mighty God (Isaiah 9:   ); so we may say, "Behold, God Himself is with us for our Captain" (2 Chronicles 13:   ).

Captain of Israel's host, and Guide
 Of all who seek the land above,
Beneath Thy shadow we abide,
 The cloud of Thy protecting love;
Our strength, Thy grace; our rule, Thy word!
Our end, the glory of the Lord.

By Thine unerring Spirit led,
 We shall not in the desert stray;
We shall not full direction need,
 Nor miss our providential way;
As far from danger as from fear,
While love, almighty love, is near.

21.

The Apostle of our Profession.

"Wherefore, holy brethren, partakers of the heavenly calling, consider the Apostle and high priest of our profession, Christ Jesus."—Hebrews 3:   .

NOW let us do what we are told, and "consider" the Lord Jesus as the Apostle of our profession. Sixteen hundred and eighty-nine years before He came, Jacob prophesied of Him as "Shiloh" (Genesis 49:   ). Shiloh means the Sent One, and "Apostle" means the same thing, "one who is sent." So when the fulness of time (that is, just the *right* time) was come, God sent forth His Son (Galatians 4:   ), sent Him to be the Saviour of the world (1 John 4:   ). The Lord Jesus seems to have delighted to remind the people that His Father sent Him, because that showed His Father's kindness and love. He said, "Neither came I of Myself, but He sent Me" (John 8:   ). See if you cannot make a list of thirty-seven verses in the Gospel of St. John, where He speaks of His Father having sent Him.

What was Jesus sent to do? He says, "Lo, I come ... to do Thy will, O God" (Hebrews 10:   ), that is, to do what God wanted Him to do. And what was that? To give Himself for our sins, that He might deliver us from this present evil world, according to the will of God and our Father (Galatians 1:   ). And He says, "This is the Father's will which hath sent Me, that of all which He hath given Me I should lose nothing." So Jesus is the Great Apostle sent with God's message of salvation to us, sent to do for us what God's loving heart wanted done, first to deliver us and then to keep us. Is not this worth "considering"?

Jesus, our Apostle, says, "as Thou hast sent Me into the world, even so have I sent them into the world" (John 17:   ). He did not mean only the eleven apostles, for He says that great prayer was *not* for them alone, but for all them which should believe on Him through their word (ver.   ). So He has sent you who believe in Jesus, just as the Father sent Him. And oh, I do so wish that some of you, some of my own dear little readers, may hear in their hearts the voice of the Lord saying, "Whom shall I send? and who will go for us?" and answer, "Here am I; send *me!*" (Isaiah 6:   ).

There are millions who have never heard the name of Jesus; would you not like to be His ambassadors to them? Will not some of you, when you are old enough, obey His command, "Go ye into all the world, and preach the gospel to every creature"? (Mark 16:   ). I think it is the greatest, grandest, noblest thing you can be, a real missionary, sent into the world by our Great Apostle!

Once a young missionary was leaving home very early in the morning. It was terribly hard work to leave his mother, and when it came to the "good-bye" his faith and courage failed; and he felt as if he could not go, and must give it up. Just that moment the hall door was opened, and all at once he caught sight of the beautiful morning star shining in the still dark sky; and instantly two texts flashed into his mind. One was, "They that turn many to righteousness shall shine as the stars for ever and ever" (Daniel 12:   ). And the other was, "I am the Bright and Morning Star!" (Revelation 22:   ). That promise of God and that bright name of Jesus shone into his heart, and gave him comfort and strength; and he went forth to the noble work.

And still God says to you all, "Who will go?"

> Who is on the Lord's side?
> Who will serve the King?
> Who will be His helpers,
> Other lives to bring?
> Who will leave the world's side?
> Who will face the foe?
> Who is on the Lord's side?
> Who for Him will go?
> By Thy call of mercy,
> By Thy grace Divine,
> We are on the Lord's side;
> Saviour, we are Thine.

22.

Our High Priest.

"We have a great High Priest."—Hebrews 4:   .

MOST likely this does not seem such an easy name as the rest; but I want you to try all the more to understand it, and be sure to find out all the texts.

St. Paul explains to us how everything that God commanded the Israelites about their worship was meant to teach something about Jesus Christ; and nearly all of it was to teach about His saving and cleansing us from sin.

Aaron was appointed the first high priest. Once every year there was to be a great day of atonement (Exodus 30:   ). Then Aaron was to kill the goat of the sin-offering (Leviticus 16:   ), and to take its blood within the veil, into the holy of holies, and sprinkle it before the mercy-seat. With this blood atonement was made for the sinful souls of the people (Leviticus 17:11 and Hebrews 9:22. Mind you look out these verses!) No one was to go in with him, and no one could help him; he was to do it all by himself. Now get the 9th chapter of Hebrews, and see how St. Paul explains it. Jesus is our High Priest (ver.   ). He did not take the blood of goats, but His own blood; and with this He entered into the holy place and obtained eternal redemption for us (ver.   ). He does not need to do it every day (Hebrews 7:   ); nor every year (Hebrews 9:   ); but once, and only once (ver.   ); because His blood is so precious that that was enough for us all and for ever (Hebrews 10:   ). No one ever had or ever can have anything to do with this great atonement by blood; it was *by Himself* that He purged our sins (Hebrews 1:   ), and by Him we have now received the atonement (Romans 5:   ). So now we may draw near, with a true heart, in full assurance of faith (Hebrews 10:   ) (that means being *quite sure*), because Jesus is our High Priest, and God's word tells us what He has done for us, so that there cannot be any mistake about it. And He is a merciful and faithful High Priest (Hebrews 2:   ), and knows all about our little feelings and temptations (Hebrews 4:   ) better than anyone else does. "Let us therefore come boldly unto the throne of grace, that we may obtain mercy and find grace to help in time of need" (Hebrews 4:   ).

23.

Wonderful.

"His name shall be called Wonderful."—Isaiah 9:   .

E VERY boy and girl knows that names are nouns. All the other names of Jesus are nouns. But here is a name that is an adjective; so we may use it not only as a name by itself, but as an adjective to all His other names; and the more we know Him and love Him, the more we shall delight in this.

If we know Jesus as our Saviour at all, we shall be quite sure that He is a Wonderful Saviour. And if we grow in grace and in the knowledge of our Lord and Saviour Jesus Christ (2 Peter 3:   ), we shall find more and more, year by year, and even day by day, what a Wonderful Friend, and Wonderful Gift, and Wonderful High Priest, and Wonderful everything else He is.

When you see a wonderful sight don't you always want others to see it first thing? And if you cannot bring them to see it, don't you want to tell about it, try to give them an idea of it? So I think one proof that we have really found Jesus is that we shall want others to come and see (John 1:   ) what a wonderful Saviour we have found.

Jesus is Wonderful in what He is. Even the angels must have wondered to see the Son of God, whom they all worship (Hebrews 1:   ), lying in a manger as a helpless and poor little baby. But I think they must have wondered more still when they saw "Him taken and by wicked hands crucified and slain" (Acts 2:   ). They must have marvelled indeed then at the love of Christ which passeth knowledge (Ephesians 3:   ), yet He was not dying for them, but for you. So the poorest little child may say, "Thy love to *me* was wonderful" (2 Samuel 1:   ).

Everything that He did was wonderful. Isaiah said that many should be astonished at Him (Isaiah 52:   ); and I want you to see how exactly that was fulfilled. Look in the first seven chapters of St. Mark, and you will see it five times mentioned that they were astonished or amazed at Him.

And His words were not less wonderful, for, as Nicodemus said, "no man ever spake like this Man" (John 7:   ). Look in the 4th chapter of St. Luke, and you will see how even those who did not love Him wondered (ver.   ), and were astonished (ver.   ) and amazed (ver.   ) at His words. If we wonder at His gracious words to us now, how much more shall we wonder when we see Him on the throne of His glory, and hear His own voice say to us, "Come, ye blessed!" (Matthew 25:   ).

O Bringer of salvation,
  Who wondrously hast wrought,
Thyself the revelation
  Of love beyond our thought:
We worship Thee, we bless Thee,
  To Thee alone we sing;
We praise Thee, and confess Thee
  Our gracious Lord and King!

24.

Counsellor.

"His name shall be called Wonderful, Counsellor."—Isaiah 9:   .

PEOPLE who think themselves very wise and clever would not care very much for this beautiful name of the Lord Jesus, for we always have to see how poor we are before we can see how precious Jesus is.

If you have found out that you are not very wise and clever, and that you sometimes make mistakes, and say or do just what you wish afterward you had not said or done, you will be ready to see how good it is to have a Counsellor.

How many foolish things we do! We have to say again and again, "O God, Thou knowest my foolishness" (Psalm 69:   ). And when we look back on a day or a week, how often we have to say, "So foolish was I" (Psalm 73:   ). Then sometimes we feel puzzled as to what we had better do, and there is no one to tell us. And sometimes we have to give an answer all in a minute, and there is no time to ask anyone to tell us what to say. These are the times for finding out what God meant by saying that "His name shall be called Counsellor." It does not take a minute to whisper to the Lord Jesus in your heart, asking Him to tell you what to do or what to say. It is not like having to write a letter to ask a friend's advice, and wait to send it by post and get an answer. The Lord Jesus is always there, and always ready to advise you.

But it is no good having a wonderful Counsellor unless you make use of Him. When the Moabites and Ammonites came against Jehoshaphat (2 Chronicles 20:   ), he said, "neither know we what to do"; but he did not stop there: he made use of the great Counsellor, and added, "But our eyes are upon Thee." And then, of course, God showed him exactly what to do, and saved him out of all the trouble. Now, the very next time you have to say, "neither know I what to do," recollect that Jesus is your Counsellor, and look up to Him, and do not be one bit afraid but what He will, in some way or other, guide you, whether it may be the steps, or the words, or anything else, that want guiding (Psalm 32:   ).

We find Jesus most of all precious as our Counsellor when we come and ask Him about the most important things of all. Sometimes we feel as if we could not possibly tell anybody what our heart is very full of, and so we go on without getting any help or counsel. Do you want to understand better about your sins being forgiven? do you want to know how to get on faster? do you want to know how to please God, and yet you have no one that you can ask about all this? Now take this name of Jesus for yourself. Jesus is come to be *your* Counsellor, and He is able to make all this clear to you far better than anyone else, if you will only ask Him. Most likely He will give you the counsel by reminding you of something that He has written already for you. He generally does this; so if you take your Bible and "watch to see what He will say unto you" (Habakkuk 2:   ), you will very soon be able to say, "I will bless the Lord who hath given me counsel" (Psalm 16:   ).

Master, speak! Thy servant heareth,
   Longing for Thy gracious word,
Longing for Thy voice that cheereth;
   Master, let it now be heard!
I am listening, Lord, for Thee;
What hast Thou to say to me?

Speak to me by name, O Master,
   Let me know it is to me;
Speak, that I may follow faster,
   With a step more firm and free,
Where the Shepherd leads the flock,
In the shadow of the Rock!

25.

The Mighty God.

"His name shall be called ... the Mighty God."—Isaiah 9:   .

C HILDREN do not often think of this name of Jesus; but it is not only the
grandest of them all, but one of the most comforting, even to a little
child who feels afraid and begins to wonder whether, after all, it will get safe to
heaven at last.

We have thought about how gracious Jesus is as our Saviour, and how lov-
ing He is as our Brother, and how kind He is as our Friend. And this is all true;
Jesus is all that; but He is more too. Now let us think of Him as the Mighty
God, and learn how great and glorious and strong our own dear Saviour and
Friend is. Now we see why He is able to do everything for us, and why He is
so mighty to save (Isaiah 63:   ). Of course He is! for this same Jesus is "the
Mighty God."

More than seven hundred years before He was born as a little child His
name was foretold; it was to be Immanuel, and that meant, God with us (Isaiah 7:   ). Then, in the next chapter, God's people were encouraged not to be
afraid, even though enemies came against them, strong and many (Isaiah 8:   ),
like the overflowing waters of a river, because of this very name, "God with us"
(ver.   ). Then, in the next chapter, more still was told about the One who was
to come, and seven names were given Him in one verse (Isaiah 9:   ).

Even Isaiah himself must have wondered what it meant (1 Peter 1:   )
when God's Spirit made him write that the coming Messiah should be "a
Child" and yet "the Mighty God." And though we do not wonder in the same
way, because we know how it came true, yet I think we shall always wonder
more and more at this mystery of godliness (1 Timothy 3:   ). How we ought
to thank God for thinking of this wonderful way of saving and helping and
meeting the children, by being God with us as a little child! And how reverently we ought to speak of the Lord Jesus when we recollect that He is "*God* our
Saviour" (Titus 1:   , 2:   , 3:   ). And oh, how sure we may be that He
must be able to save, and that we may trust Him to save us! Think of this next
time you sing, "My soul doth magnify the Lord, and my spirit hath rejoiced in
God my Saviour" (Luke 1:   ).

26.

The Everlasting Father.

"His name shall be called … the Everlasting Father."—Isaiah 9:   .

THIS is another name of Christ, of which you may not have thought. Perhaps He thought of it when He said to His disciples, "I will not leave you comfortless" (John 14:   ). For that word really means orphans, as you will see in the margin of your Bible. They could not be left orphans when Jesus was their Everlasting Father.

Perhaps some one will read this whose dear father has been taken away; possibly some one, still more to be pitied, who knows what it is to have a father without having a father's kindness and love and care. Surely this name of Jesus was meant to comfort you! Jesus, the Mighty God, is your Everlasting Father, always loving, never leaving. All that you ever knew or thought a dear father would be, He will be to you. It is those who are "without Christ" (Ephesians 2:   ) who have the saddest orphanhood; for the children of Jesus always have His promise, "I will not leave you orphans."

How did we come to be His children? This question has a wonderful answer, far away back before the world was made, farther back than you can think,—an answer which we never could have known unless He had told us Himself. We are His children, because God gave us to Jesus. For Jesus says, "Behold I and the children which God hath given me" (Hebrews 2:   ); and, "All that the Father hath given Me shall come to Me" (John 6:   ). In His great prayer for us, He speaks seven times of our being given to Him (John 17:   ). We have often thought of His being God's gift to us, but did you ever think that we are God's gift to Him? But you see He says so! So this is why we are His children, and why we are so very precious to Him. See what beautiful things we find to make us trustful and happy, when we look into His word to see what He Himself says in answer to our questions!

He is bringing many sons unto glory now (Hebrews 2:   ), and He is able to keep you from falling (Jude   ), and to present you faultless before the throne of His glory with exceeding joy. For He says, "Father, I will that they also, whom Thou hast given Me, be with Me where I am, that they may behold My glory" (John 17:   ).

"The *Everlasting* Father!"
O name of gentlest grace,
O name of strength and might,
Meeting the heart-need of our orphaned race
With tenderest delight!
Our Everlasting Father! this is He
Who came in deep humility
A little child to be!

27.

The Prince of Peace.

"His name shall be called … the Prince of Peace."—Isaiah 9:   .

SUPPOSE you go to see a grand house. The more you walk round it, inside and out, the better you will understand and admire it. But as you look first at one side and then at another, you will get quite different views of it, and yet it is always one and the same house. So it is that we get different views of the Lord Jesus, and yet He is always "this same Jesus" (Acts 1:   ).

Now, though we are right and glad to think of Jesus as King, reigning gloriously already, yet we like to remember that another of His names is Prince,— Messiah the Prince, as He was called by Gabriel (Daniel 9:   ). This shows us another side of what He is.

For a prince is a king's son, and Jesus is the Son of God, who is the King of all the earth (Psalm 47:   ).

A prince is heir to a kingdom, and so Jesus is heir of all things (Hebrews 1:   ); and the time is coming when the kingdoms of this world shall become the kingdoms of our Lord and of His Christ (Revelation 11:   ). How different the newspapers will be then, if there are any!

But a prince has royal honour now, and so it is God's will that all men should honour the Son, even as they honour the Father (John 5:   ).

A prince has other names joined to his title, and so has Jesus; and all His names show how He is the "Prince of princes" (Daniel 8:   ), far, far beyond all others.

First, He is the Prince of Peace. What music there is in this beautiful name! Does it not sound as if an echo of the angels' song had been caught and kept in it, waking up again in our hearts whenever we think of Jesus as the Prince of Peace, who made peace in heaven (Luke 19:   ) and came to give peace on earth (Luke 2:   ).

Then He is the Prince of Life (Acts 3:   ), whom God hath raised from the dead. For God has given Him power over all flesh, that He should give eternal life to as many as God has given Him (John 17:   ); and that, you know, is all who come to Him (John 6:   ).

Then He is exalted to be a Prince and a Saviour (Acts 5:   ), so that He may give repentance and forgiveness of sins.

And, last, He is the Prince of the kings of the earth (Revelation 1:   ). And this gives us a glimpse of His greatness and glory, which we do not fully see yet. But if we rejoice already in this bright and royal name of Jesus, when His glory shall be revealed we shall be glad with exceeding joy (1 Peter 4:   ).

> O the joy to see Thee reigning,
>   Thee, my own belovèd Lord!
> Every tongue Thy name confessing,
> Worship, honour, glory, blessing,
>   Brought to Thee with one accord:
> Thee, my Master and my Friend,
>   Vindicated and enthroned,
> Unto earth's remotest end
>   Glorified, adored, and owned.

28.

Messiah.

"And after threescore and two weeks shall Messiah be cut off, but not for
Himself."
—Daniel 9:   .

PERHAPS you thought this name did not sound interesting, and had nothing to do with you. Let us see!

"Messiah" is in Hebrew the same as "Christ" in Greek; and the English of
both is "Anointed." Many times in the Old Testament God speaks of Jesus as
"His Anointed." You know how kings were anointed with oil; Queen Victoria
herself was anointed with oil when she was crowned. And the high priest was
always anointed with oil when he was consecrated (Exodus 29:   ). And sometimes the great prophets were anointed before they began their work (1 Kings
19:    ). So the name "Messiah" teaches us at once that Jesus is our Prophet,
Priest, and King, all three in one.

But we never read of the Lord Jesus being anointed with oil. Oil is only a
type of something else, and not any good in itself. So we are told in plain words
that "God anointed Jesus of Nazareth with the Holy Ghost and with power"
(Acts 10:   ). Of course the Lord Jesus *as God* did not need it; for Father,
Son, and Spirit are one God. But it was *as man,* and for our sakes, that He received it; and God gave it to Him without measure (John 3:   ). Now turn
to Psalm 133, and there you will see (ver.   ) how plentifully Aaron, the high
priest, was anointed, so that the precious ointment went down from the head to
the skirts of his garments. That was to show us that the Holy Spirit, which was
poured out upon the Lord Jesus, our Head, flows down from Him even to the
feet, the lowest members of all. *Now* do you see how this name has to do with
you, if you have to do with Jesus? The blessed Spirit, whose work it is to make
us holy, is given to us because of Jesus, and comes down to us from Jesus, and
reaches in holy and constant flow every one who is joined to the Lord Jesus by
faith. There could be no gift of the Holy Spirit if it were not for the gift of Jesus, the Anointed One.

The name Messiah always reminds us, too, of God's faithfulness in sending Jesus. For it was by this name that the Jews expected Him for hundreds of
years. How glad Philip must have been when he could say, "We have found the
Messias!" (John 1:   ). Ought not we to be glad, too? For "we know that the
Son of God is come" (1 John 5:   ), and we know, too, that He is just as surely

coming again (Acts 1:   ). The Jews do not believe it even yet, because the veil is upon their heart (2 Corinthians 3:   ). They cannot make it out, because they know the time of which Daniel spoke is past long ago. We ought to pray that the veil may be taken away, that they may see that Messiah is come, and that He was cut off, not for Himself, but for them. And *for you!*

> Messiah's name shall joy impart,
> Alike to Jew and Gentile heart;
> He bled for us, He bled for you,
> And we will sing Hosanna too!

29.

Our Judge.

"He commanded us to preach unto the people, and to testify that it is He which was ordained of God to be the Judge of quick and dead."—Acts 10: .

WE must not dare to pick and choose in the Bible (Revelation 22:). It is *all* true, and will all come true; not liking to think about any part of it does not make it any the less true. Then is it not better to know the whole truth?

So, in thinking of the names of Christ, we must not leave out what seems at first sight a terrible name, for it is a great truth that He will certainly come to be our Judge. And God wishes us all to know it, for He commanded the apostles to preach it, and so His ministers would be doing wrong if they never preached about it, whether people like it or not!

"He shall come again with glory to judge both the quick and the dead." Whether we are "quick," that is "alive," when the Lord Jesus comes, or dead, will make no difference. "For we shall *all* stand before the judgment seat of Christ" (Romans 14:). There is no possibility of not having to stand there, for it says in another place "we must all appear" before it (2 Corinthians 5:). "When the Son of Man shall come in His glory, and all the holy angels with Him, then shall He sit upon the throne of His glory" (Matthew 25:). And then He will divide the sheep from the goats, and He will make no mistake. And then, surely and really, you and I will be there, standing before Him where He puts us, on the right hand or the left, and none between. And then we shall be judged out of the things that are written in the books (Revelation 21:). And nothing can possibly be hidden or forgotten then, for God says He will bring every work into judgment, with every secret thing (Ecclesiastes 12:).

Oh, how terrible, if we had never met our Judge before! No wonder that some will say to the rocks, "Fall on us!" (Revelation 6:). How shall we be able to stand in the judgment?

Stay, look at the Judge! Who is it? "Who is He that condemneth?" (that is the same word as "judgeth").

Oh, what a blessed answer! "It is Christ that died, yea rather, that is risen again, who is even at the right hand of God, who also maketh intercession for us" (Romans 8:). Now do not you see how thankful and glad we should be that *Christ* is our Judge, Christ Jesus, who came *first* to save us!

But even this would not be enough to give us confidence at His coming (1 John 2:   ). For He is "the righteous Judge" (2 Timothy 4:   ), and "will not at all acquit the wicked" (Nahum 1:   ). A *righteous* judge cannot let people off merely because they know him, or even because he loves them. Ah! but see what the Love has done! The Judge Himself has been judged in our stead, and has borne the punishment in our stead! And His righteousness is reckoned to us (Romans 3:   ). Therefore we may say:

> "Bold shall I stand in that great day,
> For who aught to my charge shall lay?
> Fully absolved through these I am,
> From sin and fear, from guilt and shame."

30.

Our Hope.

"Jesus Christ, which is our Hope."—1 Timothy 1:   .

THERE are two very different ways of using the word "hope." One is when we say "I *hope* so," with such a tone as to show that we don't very much expect so! Now if you look out all the texts about it, you will find that God never uses it that way. In His word hope always means bright, happy, confident expectation. So that must be the sort of hope He means us to have. He says, "Happy is he ... whose hope is in the Lord his God" (Psalm 146:   ).

Sometimes if we ask persons whether they are "safe in the arms of Jesus," they look very distressed, and say, "I *hope* so," with a tone that says they are very doubtful about it. That is not a bit like the bright hope St. Paul speaks of, when he says we are to "hold fast the confidence and *the rejoicing of the hope* firm unto the end" (Hebrews 3:   ).

But we can only have a bright hope by having the right hope. There is only one true hope, and that is Jesus Christ Himself. If we are "without Christ," we really have "no hope" (Ephesians 2:   ). But we need not pass another day, nor even another hour, without Him, in the dismal uncertainty of danger; you need not wait for anything at all, but at once flee for refuge to the Hope set before you, that is, to Jesus Himself (Hebrews 6:   ). And that Hope will be to you, "as an anchor of the soul, both sure and steadfast." Without it you are like a little ship driven about by the waves, and drifting every minute nearer to the rocks where she must be dashed to pieces. But with it you are like the little ship that is anchored safe on what the sailors call "good holding ground," and noth-ing can by any means hurt you (Luke 10:   ), or take away your blessed hope (Titus 2:   ). For Christ Himself will dwell in your heart by faith (Ephesians 3:   ); and He will be "in you the Hope of glory" (Colossians 1:   ); and nothing shall separate you from His love (Romans 8:   ).

> Happy, so happy! Thy Saviour shall be
> Ever more precious and present to thee,
> Onward and upward along the right way
> Lovingly leading thee day after day!

31.

Himself!

"Jesus Christ Himself."—Ephesians 2: .

YOU will say, "But this is not a name of Christ at all." Perhaps not; and yet somehow it seems to me the sweetest name of any. It is what all the other names lead up to, the reality and the crown of them all "Jesus *Himself!*" Do you know a sweeter word than that? I don't think I do! It seems to bring us right up to Him, quite close.

When the two disciples took that sorrowful walk to Emmaus, *Jesus Himself* drew near (Luke 24:); and there was no more sadness, but hearts burning within them, and the very mention of it warms our own hearts as we read. Then that same evening, when they were telling the disciples about it, "Jesus *Himself*" stood in the midst and said, "Peace be unto you!" (ver.).

It seems as if surely *any* heart must be touched, when we read again and again, "Christ also hath loved us and given *Himself* for us" (Ephesians 5:).

"Who gave *Himself* for us, that He might redeem us from all iniquity, and purify unto *Himself* a peculiar people" (Titus 2:). "Who gave *Himself* for our sins" (Galatians 1:), and, closer and more wonderful still, "gave *Himself* for *me*" (Galatians 2:). And then we read, "who *His own self* bare our sins in His own body on the tree" (1 Peter 2:). Surely He meant us to be touched and softened and won by such a word!

Then we read that because we are flesh and blood He Himself likewise took part of the same (Hebrews 2:). So that "Himself took our infirmities, and bare our sicknesses" (Matthew 8:); (ought not that to comfort the sick ones?) and He *Himself* suffered being tempted, so that He might help us when we are tempted (Hebrews 2:). There are many other places that I might tell you of, but I would rather you would try to find the rest for yourselves.

Jesus *Himself!* He Himself loves you: He Himself wants your love. It is all real and true; He Himself watches you as you read these words, and waits for your answer of love. Will not *you yourself* give yourself to Him now and for ever? He is coming again; and when He comes it will be Jesus Himself that you will see. "Whom I shall see *for myself*, and not another" (Job 19:). No! not another, not a stranger (as you will see in the margin), but "this same Jesus," "Jesus Himself." Then we shall know all the sweetness and all the glory of the reality of Jesus Christ!

He Himself, and not another,
   He who loves us to the end,
King and Saviour, Lord and Brother,
   Gracious Master, glorious Friend!

He Himself, whose name and story
   Make our hearts within us glow,
He is coming in His glory!
   Come, Lord Jesus, even so!

———

"Surely I come quickly."
         Amen.
"Even so come, Lord Jesus."
       (Revelation 22:   )

Made in the USA
Las Vegas, NV
29 July 2024

93121501R00075